# THE MAYAN
# PROPHECY 2012

# THE MAYAN PROPHECY 2012

The Mayan calendar and the end of time

David Douglas

A GODSFIELD BOOK

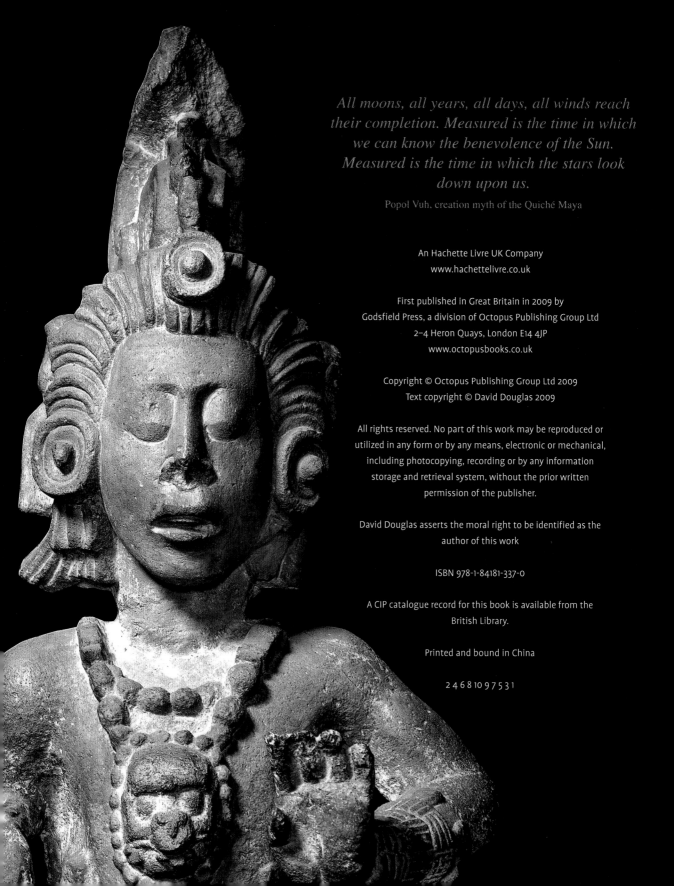

*All moons, all years, all days, all winds reach
their completion. Measured is the time in which
we can know the benevolence of the Sun.
Measured is the time in which the stars look
down upon us.*

Popol Vuh, creation myth of the Quiché Maya

An Hachette Livre UK Company
www.hachettelivre.co.uk

First published in Great Britain in 2009 by
Godsfield Press, a division of Octopus Publishing Group Ltd
2–4 Heron Quays, London E14 4JP
www.octopusbooks.co.uk

ISBN 978-1-84181-337-0

A CIP catalogue record for this book is available from the
British Library.

Printed and bound in China

2 4 6 8 10 9 7 5 3 1

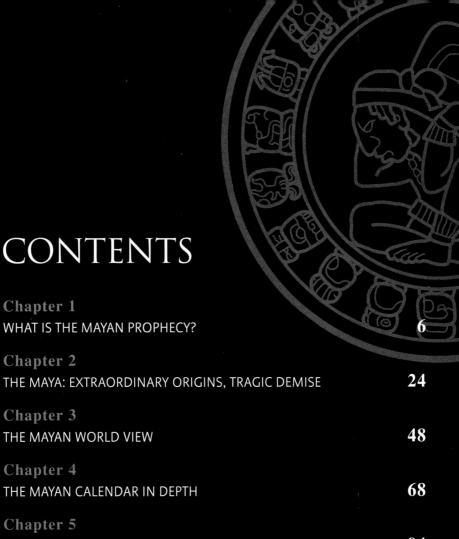

# CONTENTS

# Chapter 1

# WHAT IS THE MAYAN PROPHECY?

2012. Two thousand and twelve. Or, to be more precise, 21 December 2012 CE: 21/12/2012. The date seems to be growing in the popular imagination. People all over the world are now talking about 2012, like a spectre coming out of the fog of the future, as if to say, 'We all know that it's significant, but we're not sure what's going to happen.' So who does know – or at least claims to know – what is going to happen then? And where did this significant date come from in the first place?

It is only in the last hundred years that many of the mysteries of the Maya people of Central America have been revealed. And perhaps the greatest mystery of all has been the Long Count calendar of the Maya, which started its last Great Cycle on 13 August 3114 BCE and will come to an end 5,125 years and 132 days later on the winter solstice of 2012. While we now know that the Maya were brilliant mathematicians, astonishingly accurate astronomers and exquisitely talented artists, is it possible that they also possessed an almost supernatural foresight based on an understanding of natural cycles? Could such a civilization – which flourished more than a thousand years ago – really have predicted the end of Earth's current civilization in the second decade of the third millennium?

# Time and the Maya

*Above all, the Maya were masters of three things: time, astronomy and numbers. Of course these three aspects of life are strongly interlinked. Human beings' concepts of time have always been created from our observations of the celestial objects, and we have always needed numbers to measure the astronomical movements that make up time.*

In the years between 250 and 900 CE, the Classic Maya (as the Maya of this period were known) brought their astronomical, calendrical and mathematical understanding to an astonishingly high level. Driven by a seemingly obsessive need to understand their place in the universe and to predict their ultimate fate, the Maya recorded everything in mathematical and symbolic form. Their priest-astronomers recorded the movements of the sun, the moon, Venus, Mars and the Milky Way. At the same time, the leaders and their servants recorded the great events of their lives: births, wars, the destruction of cities, accessions and deaths.

*This Mayan calendar stone from Tikal in Guatemala depicts priests carrying out a ritual involving skulls and bones.*

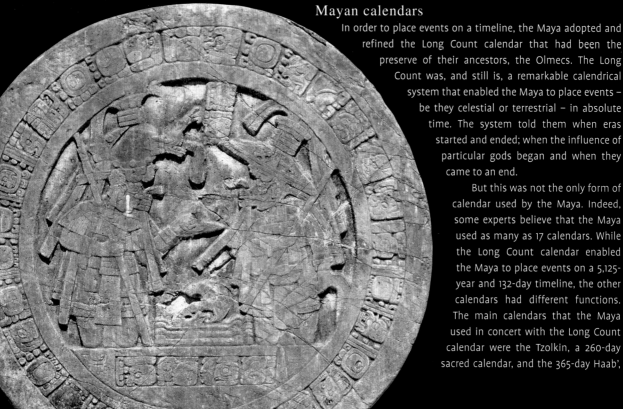

## Mayan calendars

In order to place events on a timeline, the Maya adopted and refined the Long Count calendar that had been the preserve of their ancestors, the Olmecs. The Long Count was, and still is, a remarkable calendrical system that enabled the Maya to place events – be they celestial or terrestrial – in absolute time. The system told them when eras started and ended; when the influence of particular gods began and when they came to an end.

But this was not the only form of calendar used by the Maya. Indeed, some experts believe that the Maya used as many as 17 calendars. While the Long Count calendar enabled the Maya to place events on a 5,125-year and 132-day timeline, the other calendars had different functions. The main calendars that the Maya used in concert with the Long Count calendar were the Tzolkin, a 260-day sacred calendar, and the 365-day Haab', which functioned, with regular adjustments, as a solar year like ours. The combination of the Tzolkin and the Haab' also gave rise to a 52-year cycle called the Calendar Round, at the completion of which a fire ceremony took place to ensure the continuance of time and life. At this festival the Haab' was readjusted to bring it back in line with Mayan observations, much as our leap year is used today.

This use of the 365-day Haab' as a measurement for the solar year might suggest that the Maya were not precise in their astronomy, but in fact the reverse is true. As we shall see in later chapters, Mayan observations – achieved without telescopes or other mechanical devices – were considerably more accurate than those of cultures that studied the stars many hundreds of years after the Maya.

## The planets as instruments of Fate

Their measurements were not simply a scientific project seeking knowledge for its own sake. The Maya lived in a world of religious symbol and metaphor. For them, the planets and the stars were not dead objects: they were the living embodiments of the gods, they were representatives of Mayan creative mythology and, above all, they were the forces that decided the fate of every man and woman. From their observations of the planets, the Maya would make complex and detailed prophecies for every aspect of their lives – prophecies for days, for years and for much longer periods stretching out beyond their own lives and into the future. But now their future is our present.

It comes as no surprise that the end of the Long Count calendar – which is due to take place on 21 December 2012 – was, and remains, a date of enormous significance for the Maya. It represents the culmination of the current Mayan fifth age, the completion of all cycles and the time when the gods look to make their harvest of humanity.

In the end, though, the Maya were not able to record their own swift decline. For, more rapidly than they had risen, they disappeared. In an extraordinary collapse that has left archeologists baffled, the major cities of the Maya were abandoned almost totally intact, leaving the jungles to bury the evidence. Even now, there is disagreement about the causes of their destruction: drought, wars, reproductive infertility, climate change or rapid population expansion. These and other theories are still under test, and no single answer seems to dominate. Ironically, their civilization appears to have ended before its time.

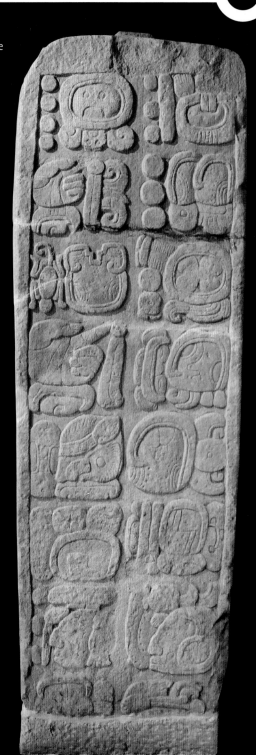

*This stela at Toniná depicts the start of the Long Count calendar – 4 Ahau 8 Kumku. This date is represented in the Gregorian calendar by 13 August 3114 BCE.*

# Apocalyptic prophecies

*The idea of end-time, apocalypse and global destruction has been with humankind since its earliest days. To talk of such endings is an expression of our mortality and the knowledge that we must all die. If people die, then worlds will die too: since stars can disappear from the heavens, we also know that our small planet spinning in space is doomed to the same fate – even if we do not know when.*

This idea of apocalypse has been expressed by nearly every major culture throughout history. Whether by flood, fire or drought, or any number of other natural manifestations, global myths of hellish endings that take everyone to their deaths in one sweep of a god's hand encapsulate our most primal fears.

The Maya people of Central America who lived in the first millennium of the Christian era were one of the most sophisticated cultures ever seen on Earth. Some of their remaining descendants, the Maya Daykeepers, still demonstrate their skill with astronomy, mathematics and prophecy today. The fifth and final age of the Mayan calendar, which started on 13 August 3114 BCE, is due to end on 21 December 2012. We know this from the relatively recent decoding of stone monuments and of the few documents, or codices (see page 43), that survived the barbaric destruction of the Spanish conquistadores in the 16th century.

## The end of the fifth age

It was, and still is, believed by the many different Maya tribes who have made their homes in Eastern Mexico, Guatemala, Honduras and El Salvador over the past 2,000 years that the fifth age of the sun will come to an end amid transformational events of a kind never witnessed on Earth before. One of the most important contemporary spiritual leaders of the Maya people is Don Alejandro Cirilo Perez Oxlaj, Head of the National Council of Elders of the Maya based in Guatemala. In their account of an interview with Don Alejandro, Patrisia Gonzales and Roberto Rodriguez report his assessment that on December 20th, 2012, the Earth would pass inside the centre of a magnetic axis, when it might be darkened with a great cloud for 60 to 70 hours and might not, due to environmental degradation, be strong enough to survive the effects. 'It will enter another age, but when it does there will be great and serious events. Earthquakes, maremotos [tsunamis], floods, volcanic eruptions and great illness on the planet Earth. Few survivors will be left.'

At the same time, Don Alejandro perceives that the year 2012 – as well as the period leading up to it – will be a time of great potential for transformation among those who choose a spiritual path.

Another positive note on the meaning of 2012 was given by a Maya-Aztec shaman named Quetza-Sha, who announced in 1991 during a total eclipse of the sun in Mexico that

a process had already started that represented the Return of Quetzalcoatl (or Kukulkán, as he was known to the Maya) – the Plumed Serpent – a major divinity in all Meso-American traditions (see page 120). This process, Quetza-Sha said, would lead to the birth of a new race in 2012: 'The year is not the destruction of the planet, but is the transformation of the spirit, sexual energy, the energy of your heart and your mind in all the dimensions of our existence in the solar system.'

## Other apocalyptic visions

The Maya are not the only people to have focused their attention around the date of 2012. There are cycles in the Tibetan, Hindu (Vedic) and Jewish calendars that indicate 2012 to be an important date. From a more prophetic standpoint, there are many native and indigenous peoples who also hold 2012 to be an important time. The Maori people of New Zealand have a legend that says the children of Tane (humankind) will be destroyed by Ranji and Papa (the sky and the earth) when they are too distracted by war and conflict to notice what is happening to them. This, it has been recently proposed by some Maori elders, will occur in 2012, when there will be a dissolving of the veil between the material and spiritual planes.

*This ornate and carefully recorded imagery is from a section of the Madrid Codex believed to date from the 15th century. Essentially a priests' manual, the Mayan codices recorded astronomical information used to maintain religious ritual and predict the future.*

## The Zulu end-time

A Zulu shaman named Credo Mutwa tells of a legend that revolves around a terrible star of the type known as Mu-sho-sho-no-no. In 1999 Mutwa described his tribe's end-time story:

> *...I am told by the great storytellers of our tribes that fresh water is not native to our Earth, that at one time, many thousands of years ago, a terrible star, or the kind called Mu-sho-sho-no-no, the star with a very long tail, descended very close upon our skies. It came so close that the Earth turned upside-down and what had become the sky became 'down', and what was the heavens became 'up'. The whole world was turned upside down. The Sun rose in the South and set in the North. Then came drops of burning black stuff, like molten tar, which burned every living thing on Earth that could not escape. After that came a terrible deluge of water accompanied by winds so great that they blew whole mountaintops away. And after that came huge chunks of ice bigger than any mountain, and the whole world was covered with ice for many generations. After that the surviving people saw an amazing sight. They saw rivers and streams of water that they could drink, and they saw that some of the fishes that escaped from the sea were now living in these rivers. That is the great story of our forefathers. And we are told that this thing is going to happen again very soon. Because the great star, which is the lava of our sun, is going to return on the day of the year of the red bull, which is the year 2012.*

*Some ancient American cultures such as the Anasazi, who built the Cliff Palace at Mesa Verde, have their own ideas about apocalyptic end-times – some of which uncannily match the predictions of the Maya.*

## Native American prophecies

There are also a number of Native American tribal peoples who look to the year 2012 as an important time of Earth changes and transformations.

The Seneca people of the Wolf Clan Teaching Lodge, the protectors of traditional Seneca medicine knowledge, have quite specific prophecies about Earth history. Grandfather Moses Shongo, who died around 1925, prophesied a period of 25 years of purification leading up to the year 2012, in which 'the Earth will purge itself'. Interestingly this period of purification, he said, would start in 1987, the year that was later identified by the writer José Argüelles (see page 132) as the time of the Harmonic Convergence, a global meditation event that was celebrated on the 16–17 August 1987 and involved hundreds of thousands of participants all around the world.

Different members of the Cherokee Nation have expressed a number of prophetic ideas about the future of the Earth. Writer and native Cherokee cultural expert Raven Hail re-presented a Cherokee calendar for our time before her death at the age of 84 in 2005. The Cherokee sacred calendar, which bears a close resemblance to that of the Maya and Aztec peoples, prophesies that this current age of the Heron (known to the Aztecs as the Sun of Movement) will end in earthquakes. Her calendar carries an end-date of 18 December 2012.

Dan Troxell, who is of 'Chickamauga Cherokee blood', describes a Cherokee calendar that functions in cycles of 1,144 years. The cycle is divided into 22 sections of 13 heavens and nine hells (an idea echoed in the Mayan calendar) and states that we are currently in a 25-year period of 'crossing', or transition, from Darkness to Light that will end in 2012 as the Earth gives birth to itself again.

## The ending of the Fourth World

The Pueblo Indians, who live in New Mexico and Arizona and are descended from the Anasazi peoples, identify themselves as Acoma, Hano, Hopi, Laguna, Navajo and Zuni. A Pueblo teacher named Speaking Wind, who died on 22 December 1998, made a number of prophecies about changes to the Earth that were already occurring, just prior to his death:

*...the final cleansing of Earth began in June 1998. In September 1998, the five brothers [planets] aligned themselves to usher in the cleansing energies of Earth. The chaos everyone has been anticipating, or the tearing away of the illusion and the lie, will begin between January and April 1999 and will continue to escalate until the nine brothers [planets] align themselves on the 5th May 2000. From that date, until the last day of the Fourth World, December 22nd 2012, a date taken from our star calendars, everything living will undergo a purge. If mankind will not willingly let go of the illusion and the lie, it will be stripped away. And we have only begun to feel the effect, since June 1998. The 23rd day of December 2012 is the first day of the Fifth World.*

The Hopi Native Americans of Arizona believe that we are living in the Fourth World out of a total of Seven Worlds or eras. They say that each of the previous three worlds ended with a cataclysmic disaster: the first ended in fire; the second era was ended when the Earth lost its balance and rotated twice, bringing floods and an age of ice; the third was ended by a flood. They say that at the end of the current world there will be a great purification, although they do not put a fixed date on when this will occur.

## Inca predictions

The Inca people of Peru and Bolivia also appear to have their own view on the 2012 date. Joan Parisi Wilcox, author of *Keepers of the Ancient Knowledge*, trained with the Q'ero priesthood in Peru and was initiated into their knowledge of prophecy concerning global spiritual evolution and our entry into a Golden Age. Unusually, their philosophy draws partly on a 16th-century Catholic idea of three ages: the age of the Father, the age of the Son and the age of the Holy Spirit. The Q'ero, who call this third age of the Holy Spirit 'Taripay Pacha', say

*Above: The Intihuatana stone (Hitching Post of the Sun) at the Incan city of Machu Picchu was used for many astronomical functions. One was to record the solar zenith, when the sun was directly overhead and cast no shadow.*

that it began during the period from 1 August 1990 to 1 August 1993, during which the planet underwent a form of transmutation called *pachakuti* or 'an overturning of space-time'. The Q'ero also say that the age of Taripay Pacha will continue until 2012, during which time humanity will evolve and a Golden Age will be initiated.

Another Inca prophecy has been put forward by a descendent of the Quechua nation named Willaru Huayta, who says that the Inca calendar will end in 2013, when a 'huge magnetic asteroid' three times the size of Jupiter will pass close to Earth. His prophecy states that the ensuing cataclysm will destroy most of humankind, save for a few who will become the 'seed people' of the Sixth Generation. Huayta suggests that those who work to overcome their egos and heal their spiritual sickness may be able to join this select group.

## Interpreting the prophecies

So what do all these prophecies – both negative and positive – mean? Should we be afraid, daunted or excited? How should we prepare for such events? What do such times demand of us, both as individuals and as a race that has responsibility for this planet called Earth? And are there any connections between what is being described and the kind of changes being brought about by environmental destruction?

Before we try to answer these difficult and challenging questions, perhaps we should look at the scientific evidence that already exists about the processes that might drive such changes.

*Opposite: The astronomical observatory at Machu Picchu. Like the Maya, the Inca and their descendants have prophecies, based on astronomical calculations, that concern 2012 and the ending of the current age.*

# Sunspots, solar flares and magnetic-field changes

*In the last 20 years there has been a massive increase in the number of scientific studies predicting that climate change will have huge repercussions for life on this planet. But if these changes are purely man-made, how is it possible – as some say the Mayan calendar suggests – that they are part of natural cycles that would lead to cataclysm? There is certainly a vocal minority of scientists who still hold that the most potent forces that cause major conflagrations and global disasters are actually driven by the cycles of the sun, rather than by human interaction with the natural world.*

### Solar cycles and sunspot activity

The most recent research into solar cycles and, in particular, sunspot activity has come to conclusions that may have a bearing on events in 2012. Sunspots are the dark areas on the sun that appear when lines of magnetic force close to the star's outer layer manage to pierce the surface on their way out and on their return. As these events occur, they liberate solar flares and 'coronal mass ejections', both of which throw out radiation and charged particles towards the Earth. These solar storms can disrupt the Earth's atmosphere, cause satellite and electrical failures and, if some experts are to be believed, drive drought cycles and even fertility cycles in humans and other mammals.

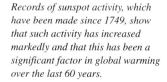

*Records of sunspot activity, which have been made since 1749, show that such activity has increased markedly and that this has been a significant factor in global warming over the last 60 years.*

The main solar cycle that scientists study is approximately 11 years long and is called the Schwabe cycle. As well as recording peaks of solar activity, it also measures the period in which the sun reverses its magnetic poles. There are also longer cycles, such as the 208-year Suess cycle and the 2,300-year Hallstatt cycle, that record longer periodic fluctuations. The Suess cycle in particular has been closely correlated with major climatic changes, including high incidences of drought.

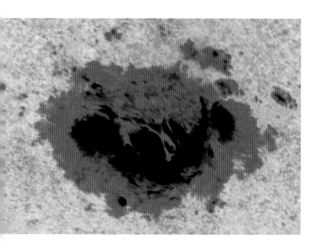

### Record-breaking solar events of 2001 onwards

With the growing research focus on climate change, scientific study of sunspot activity has also increased in recent years and has now been linked by some researchers to a number of factors affecting life on Earth, including the fertility of plants and humans. This rise in interest has been partly due to a very large solar-flare event that happened in early 2001. Normally, about 11 years pass before activity within the sun changes from one hemisphere to the other. In line with this predicted cycle, a major event was due in March/April 2000, although in reality it

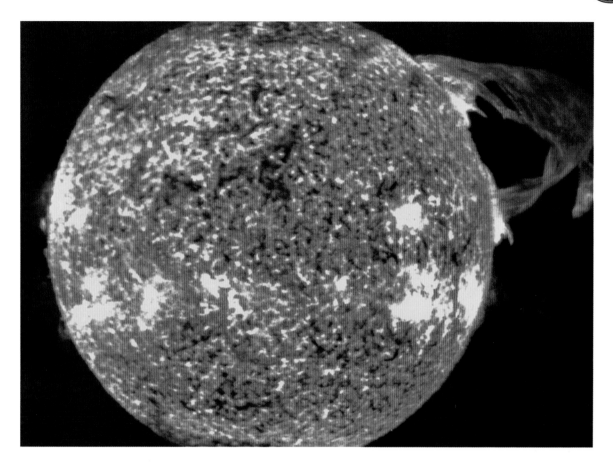

did not start to peak until February 2001. In April 2001 a record-breaking solar flare hit the Earth, exceeding the then-maximum of X-20 on the measurement scale for such events. George Withbroe, Scientific Director of NASA's Sun–Earth Connection Programme, claimed, 'This is a unique solar maximum in history. The images and the data are beyond the wildest expectations of the astronomers of a generation ago.'

But Withbroe's assessment would soon be outdated. In the following 30 months an unprecedented series of events occurred. In June 2001 the Aurora Borealis, normally only visible in high latitudes close to the Arctic Circle, was seen as far south as Mexico. Then, in 2002, the gaseous envelope of the sun ruptured, in an event known as a coronal mass ejection (CME). This particular CME was the most complex ever witnessed by scientists. The year 2003 brought even more surprises: nine huge solar eruptions took place in just 12 days – a previously unheard-of manifestation. But then, on 4 November 2003, an even more shocking event occurred: the largest single solar flare ever witnessed by scientists. At the time it was thought to have been between X-28 and X-35 on the scale that measures the intensity of solar radiation, but it is now thought to have been even larger. It knocked out many electronic and satellite systems, causing radio blackouts and grid overloads and establishing a new level for the damaging potential of solar activity.

*This NASA image shows a 'coronal mass ejection' or solar-flare event. These occur at regions of the sun's surface where intense magnetic activity occurs. Some scientists believe that the increasing ferocity of solar discharges could be responsible for major disasters on Earth.*

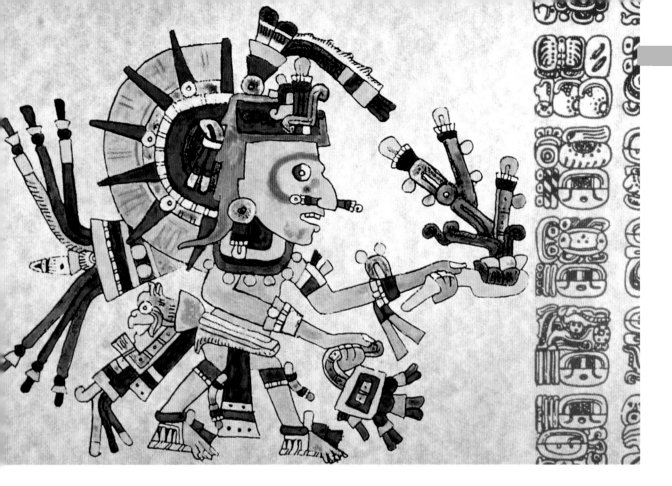

*The sun god was a powerful presence in all pre-Columbian cultures. The Aztec calendar depicts the sun god Tonatiuh, whom they considered the ruler of the current age of the Fifth Sun.*

## Cotterell's theories

This overall increase in solar activity is worrying scientists, who see that the current levels of solar activity are the highest for around 8,000 years. It is also concerning those looking at the Mayan calendar and its implications. Scientist and Mayan researcher Maurice Cotterell has been studying the effects of sunspot activity on humans since his 1988 book *Astrogenetics*. However, in 1995 he became more closely linked to the idea that 2012 represented a major solar event that would lead to a shift in the Earth's magnetic poles, a series of natural disasters and significant changes in humans' ability to reproduce. In his well-known book *The Mayan Prophecies*, co-written with Adrian Gilbert, Cotterell put forward detailed ideas about how the effects of long-term sunspot cycles over periods of thousands of years have already brought to an end previous cultures through the same cyclical process, with each of these events severely diminishing human fertility.

Cotterell also foresaw a link between solar magnetic cycles and magnetic activity within the Earth itself. He is not alone in believing that the Earth is due for a reversal of its magnetic polarity – an event that has occurred many times in its history and that may have been linked to other devastating effects. There is significant disagreement within the scientific community as to how often this has occurred in 'deep' history, but general consensus sees the last reversal – known as the Brunhes-Matuyama reversal – as having taken place about 780,000 years ago. It has now been discovered that the Earth's current magnetic-field strength is diminishing very quickly, having declined by about 15 per cent in the past 150 years. The scientific establishment agrees that if the current rate of reduction continues, a collapse of the Earth's magnetic fields could occur within a few hundred years. If, however, the rate of decline accelerates further, we may see such an event much sooner, as Maurice Cotterell believes. If this happens, there are a number of possible effects – some of which may lead to what the experts politely term 'biological extinction'. We might prefer to call it 'the end of human life.'

## Peacock's predictions

An interesting confirmation of changing solar processes has come from an Australian radio ham called Kevin Peacock, after noticing that the quality of his radio signals was being affected by solar activity. Having made this observation, Peacock undertook a thorough study of solar activity over the nearly 400 years in which it has been recorded. As well as confirming the notion that solar activity has been on the increase, Peacock went on to study the correlation between solar, geomagnetic and seismic activity. He came to the conclusion that in June and July 2011 four factors could potentially coincide to create a cataclysmic event. The four events capable of bringing about such a collapse are as follows:

- The summer solstice on 21 June 2011 means that the North Pole will be closest to the sun at that point.

- Three eclipses (two solar, one lunar) will occur between 2 June and 1 July 2011, initiating geomagnetic effects.

- A solar-flare event is due to occur in which the sun's magnetic field reverses.

- A larger cycle of solar activity – which has been on the increase for many years – will also peak at around this time.

It is Peacock's contention that such a concordance of events has not occurred for 65 million years and that it will cause the Earth's magnetic field to collapse and reverse, leading to 'earthquake and volcano activity bringing about the end of our civilization by the end of 2012'.

The sun, which the Maya and so many other cultures have worshipped as the source of all life, may become our nemesis.

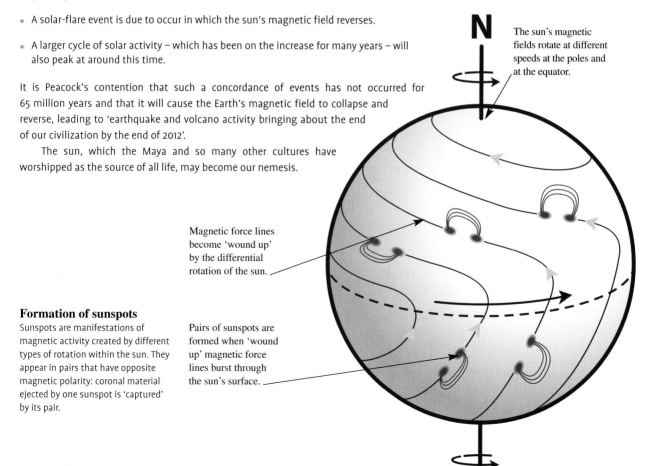

N

The sun's magnetic fields rotate at different speeds at the poles and at the equator.

Magnetic force lines become 'wound up' by the differential rotation of the sun.

### Formation of sunspots

Sunspots are manifestations of magnetic activity created by different types of rotation within the sun. They appear in pairs that have opposite magnetic polarity: coronal material ejected by one sunspot is 'captured' by its pair.

Pairs of sunspots are formed when 'wound up' magnetic force lines burst through the sun's surface.

# Environmental apocalypse

*Over the past 30 years increasing amounts of scientific data have confirmed that the human race has been causing changes to the Earth's self-regulating system that may lead to irreversible environmental damage. Each month seems to bring ever more worrying prognoses for the deteriorating condition of the planet.*

Groups such as the IPCC (Intergovernmental Panel on Climate Change), formed in 1988, have done more than most to draw attention to the growth in atmospheric $CO_2$ levels that threaten to end the self-regulating stability of our climate. Ex-US Vice-President Al Gore's 2006 film, *An Inconvenient Truth*, had a huge and frightening impact on many people who had previously believed that climate change was none of their business. In 2007 Ban Ki-moon, Head of the United Nations, speaking about the Earth's problems announced, 'We are all in this together – we must work together.' However, with increasing energy demands in the Western world and China's rapid expansion being fuelled by hundreds of new coal-fired power stations, hopes of reducing the emissions that are destabilizing the planet remain very small.

## Early warnings

Looking back to earlier times, it is easy to believe that the unusual and more extreme weather conditions that we are now experiencing could not have been predicted by our forefathers. The fossil-fuel revolution started in earnest during the nineteenth century, but few people of the time had any idea that human activity could damage the environment in any substantial or irreversible way. Surely the world was big enough not to have to worry about our impact on it?

In truth, however, there have always been voices warning of the dangers inherent in our combustion technologies. Even Nikola Tesla, the man who gave the world AC or 'alternating current' technology, and who started the major long-distance electrification of North America when he used Niagara Falls to produce electricity, warned of the risks. Speaking in 1890 he told the world, 'we should be able to produce our electrical energy without the consumption of fuels'.

His voice was one of just a few that predicted the dangers of technologies based on combustion. The last 100 years have been a story of unfettered growth, undiminished expansion and exponentially increasing pollution of the world's atmosphere.

*Water levels in China's major rivers, such as the Jialing, have reached near-record lows due to unusually warm temperatures. Over five million Chinese people face drinking-water shortages.*

## Mayan foresight and precedent

So is it possible that these self-destructive activities are in some way linked to the predictions of the Maya? After all, the Maya may have experienced their own localized climate-change problems. Or is the cataclysmic environmental change brought about by humans' combustion of fossil fuels simply a coincidence with destructive events that are part of other cycles? It seems an unlikely synchronicity that the Maya should have predicted the end of an era that humanity is now bringing about by its own hand, using technologies that were not even imagined 5,000 years ago.

Most people view our carelessness of the environment, and our seeming inability to change our habits of wasteful energy use, as the driver of our global nightmare. However, there are more controversial theories that see a different psychological process at work. Given that we have all the information we could possibly need about the results of our careless behaviour, could our headlong rush towards disaster be a self-fulfilling prophecy, driven by a reckless, subconscious belief in 'end-time' and an internal sense of its inevitability? Or are we so blinded by our need for economic growth, increasing profits and the relentless processing of natural resources that to stop the process would bring about a different kind of human disaster, driven by economic implosion?

Interestingly, many scholars believe that the Maya may also have valuable lessons to teach us about the progress of civilization. The rapid collapse of the Maya seems to have been brought about in part, at least, by environmental mismanagement. Studying the Maya may help us avoid a similar fate.

## A chance to redeem ourselves

It would be ironic to think that the very progress we believe in, the evolution we pride ourselves on, could actually be the cause of our downfall. And yet that is what many now believe is happening. So we have, as a race, a choice: to wake up to the consequences of our actions and the need to change our lives, in order to rescue ourselves from ourselves; or to ignore what we see around us. Only through a huge effort of will on a collective basis can we reverse the damage we are creating. And the ones who will thank us will be future generations.

*Sea levels are set to change markedly over the next centuries, reducing land areas available for human activity and displacing many people from their homes.*

# The Mayan prophecy: disaster or awakening?

*To some experts it seems that the Maya lived through a miniature version of the world's current environmental crisis. They faced the same disaster and the same choices. It may not have destroyed their whole planet, but it appears, on the balance of evidence, to have ended their civilization. What then do we have to learn from them – from both their wisdom and their failure?*

*Even at major Mayan sites, such at Tikal in Guatemala, many of the temples and other buildings lie buried beneath dense foliage – the result of over 1,000 years of growth since their abandonment.*

The Maya had a picture of life driven by sacred cycles of time. They believed that their people had undergone four previous cataclysms in which the great majority had perished. They also believed that enough of them had survived these disasters to make it possible to continue their culture. It was their firm belief that the fifth Great Cycle, which started in the year we call 3114 BCE, would come to an end on 22 December 2012 CE, on the day they call 12.19.19.17.19 in their Long Count calendar. For the Classic Maya, who lived between 250 and 900 CE, there was little sign that they believed in any future material reality beyond this end-date.

## The benefits of hindsight

At the same time, their culture all but disappeared within the space of a few hundred years, between 700 and 1000 CE. Like poor clairvoyants, they don't seem to have seen the coming of their own end. If we could talk to them now, what would they tell us? That they underestimated their own need for power over their enemies? That they misunderstood the pressures which the rise of their civilization was putting on the environment that supported them? That their rulers neglected the needs of the ordinary people? Or were there other, more mysterious reasons for their demise? Whatever the answers, they might sound terrifyingly familiar to our contemporary world.

What then are we to make of their prediction that this age will come to an end? Are we to believe the evidence that celestial cycles will cause such changes in the Earth's magnetic field that a series of disasters will overwhelm the majority of humankind? Are we the generation who will finally face a major global conflagration that will reverse the technological advances of the past 200 years and leave us naked in the face of overwhelming natural forces?

Will the events of 2012 be some kind of cosmic 'sorting process', which could intelligently remove those who have failed to respect the planet and save a favoured few who will go forth and multiply, repeopling a slowly recovering planet with a more enlightened DNA pool? Or will the damage be more random – just as Fate's hand seems, to many, to act cruelly and irrationally?

For some people, whether we live or die is not the ultimate question. The greater question is whether we – both as individuals and as a group – can respond to the spiritual challenges that such disasters pose and develop our spirits, or souls, in connection with the Intelligent Force behind all creation.

### What the Mayan prophecy tells us

This book explores every aspect of Mayan prophecy and its implications for us all. Chapter 2 puts the Maya in context, exploring their origins, society and decline. Chapter 3 looks at the Mayan world view, examining their spirituality and mythology and how the Mayan prophecy fitted into their own concept of the universe.

The extraordinary achievement of the Mayan calendar is analysed in depth in Chapter 4, which looks at how the Maya measured time so accurately and at how the recording of time was, for them, a sacred process. Chapter 5 demonstrates just how sophisticated and accurate Mayan observations were, and examines the implications of this for the accuracy of their prophecies.

The meaning and messages of the calendar and the views of other spiritual leaders form the subject of Chapter 6. And, finally, Chapter 7 looks at the future – what can we conclude from the evidence of the Mayan prophecy?

# Chapter 2

# THE MAYA: EXTRAORDINARY ORIGINS, TRAGIC DEMISE

There are two significant stories about the Maya. There is their own ancient story – of the rise of their remarkable culture – and there is the modern story of how scientists, scholars and experts in different fields have made a seemingly endless series of breathtaking discoveries that have gradually revealed more of the true nature of the Maya and the body of knowledge that was uniquely theirs.

Early Europeans knew that the Maya were related to their Meso-American 'cousins', the Aztecs, but did not know or understand the links between the different strands of development that had occurred over many thousands of years. For the most part, the Catholic conquistadores were intent on suppressing any resistance to their total domination of all they encountered. The 'savage Indians' were there to be saved from themselves for the glory of a Christian God – whether or not He desired it. However, knowledge of the roots of the Maya has gradually emerged to tell a fascinating and surprising story that, even now, continues to throw up new and extraordinary facts. It is these facts that help us appreciate the achievements of the Maya and understand how they might have comprehended the world in ways that we can still only dream of.

# Mayan society and culture

*Mayan culture, as it manifested itself during the Classic period between 250 and 900 CE was one of the most sophisticated cultures ever to have graced the planet. Not only were the Maya advanced for their own time, but there are aspects of their mathematics, architecture, astronomy, art, language and writing that are still to be bettered by modern global society with its huge advantages in technology.*

How was this possible? How can a culture rise so spectacularly and produce so many new ideas, novel achievements and fresh insights? Was it through the work of a few exceptional geniuses – the Leonardos, Brunelleschis and Einsteins of their time, who made paradigm-shifting discoveries? Or was it more of a collaborative work that involved different levels of society? And how did their spiritual knowledge help, or hinder, their achievements?

### Decoding the Mayan mysteries

Because Mayan language was so deeply encoded in their hieroglyphics – hieroglyphics that captured both their language and their ideas about time and cycles – we are only now unravelling many of the greatest mysteries of the Maya people. However, some important work has been done to uncover key figures in Mayan history, to reveal important social developments that took place in Mayan life over many hundreds of years, and to understand the philosophical and intellectual sources for their way of life.

What is remarkable about the Maya is the way in which so many aspects of their lives were highly integrated. It is difficult for the modern mind to appreciate fully just how deeply a sense of intellectual and spiritual order permeated their whole world. The threads of their spirituality, their mathematics, their sense of time – as expressed through the calendars – and their cosmology were enmeshed as in the most harmonious and patterned fabric, which encoded their deepest beliefs about their own destiny.

### Mayan society

At the same time, their social cohesion and sense of their own great destiny relied on a very hierarchical and often violent social structure. The ruling class in each city of the many city-states spread across the Mayan world was supported by a large population of farmers, who provided the food resources for the ever-growing numbers of people. There is still some disagreement about just how they achieved such high productivity, but there is strong evidence that they used sophisticated water-management methods and created terracing, canal systems and reservoirs, as well as drained and raised fields.

The Maya appear to have used rotational agricultural systems that allowed them to utilize their land from year to year, rather than the simpler slash-and-burn techniques of monoculture, which yields increasingly poor crops. As well as their staple of maize, the Maya grew varieties of squash and pumpkin and two types of bean – one red, one black. They also grew chillies, which provided an important flavour in their cooking.

They also seem to have used 'forest garden' methods that involved a 'three-dimensional' use of fields to grow trees and larger plants. These would have fixed nitrogen in the soil and provided shade for smaller, energy-rich plants such as the cacao plant, which brought them the luxury of chocolate. This way of growing crops was productive in many ways: the shelter trees planted for the cacao also provided the Maya with building and thatching materials, as well as animal fodder, medicines, wood and fruit. It was a carefully maintained ecosystem that maximized the yield from the cacao crop.

## Water shortages

At every turn, it seems that the Maya were more sophisticated than we may first have thought. This did not, however, make their civilization invincible. The fact that fresh water usually remained stubbornly 150 metres (500 feet) below ground meant that water management was absolutely critical. It seems likely that, ultimately, it was the inaccessibility of this source of life that contributed to the collapse of the Maya.

The rise of the Maya was at least as spectacular as their fall, and while it may be easy to look at their demise and imagine – with wise hindsight – how they might have prevented it, we may do better to look at our own situation and search for parallels. Many people now wonder whether the Maya, who could not foresee their own first-millennium downfall, may have more accurately predicted ours.

*Opposite: Represented as both male and female, the Mayan maize god was considered to be the father of the Hero Twins in the Popol Vuh, the most important creation myth of the Maya.*

*Below: This panel, known as the Lápida DuPaix and discovered in the 19th century, commemorates an event in the life of K'inich Janaab' Pakal, ruler of Palenque, which took place on the Long Count date of 9.11.1.0.0.*

# Who were the Maya?

*It seems strange to think that the city of Palenque, possibly the greatest of all the architectural and cultural achievements of the Maya people, was only revealed to European explorers in 1773. Its step pyramids, temples and palaces – the evidence of an extraordinarily developed society – had lain buried in deep jungle for hundreds of years following the collapse of Mayan society around 1000.*

*The huge carved heads pre-date Mayan culture and have led researchers to speculate about the racial origins of the early American peoples, with some writers claiming these could be African or Egyptian.*

Perhaps even more astonishing is the fact that only now, in the 21st century, is the story of the Maya people and their rise and fall being fully decoded and understood by the small cohort of Mayanists and scholars who have dedicated their lives to unveiling the knowledge possessed by these remarkable people. Before we can fully understand and appreciate the Maya, however, it is necessary to take a broader look at the different peoples who inhabited pre-Hispanic Meso-America – the area now occupied by Mexico, Guatemala, Belize, El Salvador and parts of western and southern Honduras.

## The Olmec people

It is widely understood that the earliest influential culture in Meso-America comprised the Olmec people. They were originally believed to have developed in the tropical lowlands of southern Veracruz and adjacent Tabasco as far back as 3000 BCE. In valleys and coastal lowlands they started to grow crops of maize, their main staple, as well as beans and squash. From around 2500 BCE pottery started to appear, and by 1500 BCE they were living in villages. Around 1200 BCE the Olmecs were building ornate pyramids from mud bricks, few of which have survived the ravages of time. At the same time they started to carve in basalt: figures and large heads, some 3 metres (10 feet) tall, representing their gods and rulers. They also invented the famous Meso-American ball-game, which was played in many forms and under a variety of brutal rules (for a more detailed description, see page 61).

The Olmecs are also thought to be the source for the basic elements of the sacred Mayan calendar. Until recently the earliest example of stone stelae (upright stone slabs) bearing dates in the Long Count calendar form was found in the Olmec village now called Tres Zapotes. Stela C, as it is called, bears a Long Count calendar date of 7.16.3.2.13 or 36 BCE. Since that discovery a stela four years older has been unearthed at Chiapa de Corzo in Mexico's Chiapas region.

Major Mayan sites
1 Dzibilchaltun
2 Mayapan
3 Chichén Itzá
4 Tulum
5 Uxmal
6 Kabah
7 Sayil
8 Labna
9 Jaina Island
10 Hochob
11 Chicanna
12 Cerros
13 Calakmúl
14 El Mirador
15 Nakbé
16 Uaxactun
17 Holmul
18 Buenavista
19 Naranjo
20 Tikal
21 Yaxha
22 Tayasal
23 Piedras Negras
24 Yaxchilán
25 Bonampak
26 Altar de Sacrificios
27 Seibal
28 Palenque
29 Comalcalco
30 Nebaj
31 Izapa
32 Quirigua
33 Copán

## Zapotec constructions

The Olmecs seem to have begun a series of migrations that eventually resulted in the development of various strands of Meso-American culture, including the Toltecs and the Maya. One of their migrations saw a move west to the area around Oaxaca, where they started to occupy what is now known as the plateau of Monte Alban. Between 800 and 300 BCE they built a series of important structures, including pyramids, some of which survive today. By 400–300 BCE the Zapotec people had taken over Monte Alban and had started to build over the Olmec structures. At this time the first signs of writing forms appeared. New pyramids were constructed, often linked by subterranean passageways. The Zapotecs also created an innovative system for collecting rainwater: their central plaza – as large as two football pitches – was built with a slight camber, or curve, so that all the water that fell on

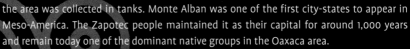

the area was collected in tanks. Monte Alban was one of the first city-states to appear in Meso-America. The Zapotec people maintained it as their capital for around 1,000 years and remain today one of the dominant native groups in the Oaxaca area.

Within the Mayan area to the east, pottery and the creation of villages seem to have begun around 1000 BCE, with larger, more 'civic' buildings appearing from 500 BCE onwards. Here writing started in about 400 BCE.

## Aztec civilization

In what is now called the Proto-Classic period between 100 BCE and 250 CE there was a rise in complex urban cultures across all of Meso-America. While Zapotec development was occurring in the Oaxaca area, further west the place that would become the great centre of Aztec civilization – Teotihuacán – was under construction. The massive Pyramid of the Sun was started there around the beginning of the Christian era. At its height, under the Aztecs of the second millennium, this great centre of civilization would cover 20 sq km (8 sq miles) and boast a population of some 200,000 people.

## The flowering of Mayan art

During the Proto-Classic period, in the eastern parts of Meso-America area now thought of as the world of the Maya, city-states such as Abaj Takalik, Izapa, El Mirador, Kaminal-juyu, Uaxactun and Tikal began to emerge. Their lords and rulers began the building of monumental art and architecture – some clearly showing episodes in mythological stories. Of the roughly 15,000 inscriptions so far discovered on Mayan stonework and pottery, the content solely concerns the kings and leaders of the states and their victories in battle, while the ordinary people did not feature in this written history.

As the peasant economies became more sophisticated and provided resources for the growing population, so the city rulers' ambitions began to gather momentum. How the art, architecture, mythology and spirituality of the Maya grew and developed alongside this economic development is not precisely known, but the evidence of this extraordinary flowering, during what is known as the Classic Maya period of 250–900 CE, is still being revealed today.

Judging by the increase in archeologically recorded house sites, monuments and other buildings, together with Long Count calendar dates that reveal the age of certain events, the absolute peak of Mayan civilization occurred during the 8th century. At this time there are estimated to have been millions of people in the many Mayan city-states across eastern Meso-America. Within just another 200 years, however, the last-recorded Long Count date was carved in stone at the city of Toniná close to Palenque. In our calendar it was 18 January 909. The most highly developed society of the entire American continent had imploded.

# The Mayan city-state

*It is important to remember that the entire architectural achievement of the Maya appears to have been manifested without the wheel, without beasts of burden for pulling, without metal tools and without the use of pulleys. What the Maya had in place of some of these technologies was people – and many of them – and their rulers worked them hard to create sacred places where rituals could be enacted.*

*Opposite: Its massive Jaguar temple dominating the central square, Tikal epitomizes the power of the Mayan city-state. The city, which covers a huge area and whose remains span a long historical period, has yet to yield up all its secrets.*

*Below: Dramatic geometric mosaics at Mitla in the state of Oaxaca were created with small, interlocking pieces of limestone. They are believed to represent deities and the natural elements.*

*America, say historians, was peopled by savages; but savages never reared these structures; savages never carved these stones.*

John Stephens, Copán, 1839

## Mayan architecture

Even with the rise in manpower facilitated by booming populations, the evolution of Mayan architecture appears to have been a remarkably swift development. From the basic homes of the Pre-Classic periods, the relatively sudden appearance of monumental architecture has surprised many archeologists. Also of great interest to scientists is the question of just how independent Mayan ideas were. Could they really have developed their own style of architectural expression without the influence of Teotihuacán and Aztec culture, or was their development an evolution of ideas from Olmec and Zapotec sources? Recent research has focused on the influential arrival of powerful warlords from Teotihuacán in the 4th century. One leader in particular, a man named Fire is Born, may have played an influential role in the cultural, political and artistic development of the Maya. However, there are monumental pyramids at Tikal – perhaps the largest of all Mayan cities – that originate from the 3rd century and testify to the architectural impulses of the early Maya.

Many of the great Mayan cities followed similar patterns in their development and had a number of common features that are unique to the Maya, and which enabled them to pursue their particularly ritualized lives. Of all the sites in Meso-America, probably the most significant, most famous and most revealing are those at Tikal, Palenque, Chichén Itzá, Uxmal, Copán, Calakmul and Mayapán.

## Location and water sources

Sites for the major Mayan cities vary enormously, according to the topography of the local area. In the northern Yucatán, Chichén Itzá was created on a flat limestone plain, where room for

*Calakmul was the major seat of power of the Ka'an people, also known as the Kingdom of the Snake. Calakmul's 45-metre (148-foot) pyramid known as Structure 2, viewed here from its summit, is the largest Classic-era temple platform in the Mayan world.*

expansion was available and large populations could coalesce around the city centre. In the jungle highlands, however, such as those around Palenque, the hilly landscape dictated a different approach, which used the natural features as platforms for the most important Mayan temples and palaces and enabled them to build soaring edifices that became important landmarks visible for many miles. Often the roof combs that topped the temples contained images of their rulers.

Before the Maya first started to build their cities, they would usually seek out substantial fresh-water wells called *cenotes*, which could provide a large part of their water needs. These naturally occurring water-holes are still an important part of the Mayan landscape.

## City construction

The great majority of the Yucatán peninsula area is formed from limestone and the Mayan architecture of the region used this quarried limestone as its major raw material. The Maya created a form of mortar or cement made from crushed and burned limestone. This was also used as 'limestone-stucco', which could be modelled into reliefs and decorative patterns and provide a smooth and even covering.

Initial buildings at the heart of their city centres would be oriented according to the four major directions, a key principle in Mayan culture and spirituality. Virtually all Mayan cities were focused on a large plaza, around which the major ceremonial and governmental buildings were erected. They were often dominated by step pyramids, each of which was topped with a temple where calendrical ceremonies – some of them involving sacrifice – were carried out. Some cities, such as Tikal, also contained a royal acropolis and/or royal palaces, and ritual ball-courts were sometimes a central feature of the plaza.

## Solar and lunar alignment

Mayan cities tended to grow up organically. Unlike the great Aztec cities, which were laid out on fixed grid patterns with everything in its allotted place, Mayan city-states, which evolved and were remodelled or rebuilt over time, tended to be more random in their layout. There are, however, many examples of sets of buildings being laid out to provide observational references for solar, lunar and other celestial events. Some of these are called E-groups, such as the archetypal example at Uaxactun, named Structure E-VII-sub. These are generally formed of a main stepped pyramid temple on the west side of a plaza, together with further smaller temples in the northern and southern quadrants, opposite the main temple. Often the principal western structure has several levels, and just one staircase on its eastern side to allow access from the main plaza. Typically the stairways have substantial balustrades that project from the pyramid and carry stucco masks and reliefs. This layout enabled priests to carry out observations of the sun's equinoxes and solstices, using smaller subsidiary buildings as 'siting' objects for solar and lunar events.

At Copán, the 72 steps of the Hieroglyphic Stairway are carved with more than 1,250 hieroglyphs telling the story of 15 of the city's rulers up to 755 CE. When it was first discovered, the stone blocks of the stairway were scattered around the site, but archeologists have worked to reassemble the stairway in the correct order and uncover the royal history of this major site.

## The discovery of Calakmul

Calakmul is another large city-state deep in the jungles of the Petén Basin region of Guatemala. Like many Mayan sites, its discovery was relatively recent; biologist Cyrus L. Lundell of the Mexican Exploitation Chicle Company discovered evidence of the site from the air on 29 December 1931. Calakmul, which means City of the Two Adjacent Pyramids, was actually the name given to the city by Lundell himself. After an initial exploration by Sylvanus Morley in 1932, the site was left unattended until 1984, when a detailed ten-year study of it started.

More than 6,250 structures have so far been discovered in an area of some 70 sq km (27 sq miles), of which a central, more intensely populated area was around 22 sq km (8½ sq miles). Here scientists have revealed the largest-known constructed reservoir of the Mayan world. It is thought that, at its height, the city was able to support a population of around 50,000 people. Calakmul was established as the main centre of the Ka'an, or Kingdom of the Serpent, and the people here were allies of Caracol, a rival to the city of Tikal. Architecturally Calakmul is particularly interesting for its 45-metre (148-foot) pyramid known as Structure 2, which is the single largest Classic-era temple platform in the whole of the Mayan world.

*Sacred wells or* cenotes *provided important sources of water for city-states. Recent discoveries of human skulls and bones have revealed that they were also used as places of sacrifice.*

# Anatomy of a city: Copán

*This reconstruction of Copán suggests how a typical Classic-period ceremonial centre might have appeared, with its stepped platforms topped with towering temple-pyramids and broad plazas. The exterior façade of these structures would have been embellished with colourful painted stucco reliefs.*

The buildings surrounding the plazas, often called palaces, were administrative centres. Seated on benches covered with jaguar skins, the city's ruler would receive tributes, make judicial rulings and entertain visitors. In the courtyards more public activities, such as sacred dances, blood-letting and prisoner sacrifices, took place. At the city's height, at about 800 CE, some 20,000 people lived in Copán and its vicinity. Food for the city was produced in rural settlements in the Copán River valley.

## 1 Acropolis
Copán's main structural grouping is the Acropolis, overlooking the Copán River. Over time the Acropolis was added to and remodelled, with new structures built over old ones.

## 2 Hieroglyphic Stairway
This grand staircase leading up to the Acropolis from the west was built in its current form by Copán's 13th ruler, Uaxaclajuun Ub'aah K'awiil (18 Rabbit), in the early 8th century. Its inscriptions record the birth, parentage, accession to power, important achievements and death of the most distinguished rulers of the city.

## 3 Popul Nah
The Popul Nah, or Council House, is sometimes called the Great Mat House because enormous mats of mosaic stone decorated the building. On the upper wall are portraits of Mayan lords seated on glyphs that may represent the locality they governed. Meetings were held under the sun and stars on the wide porch in front of the structure, rather than inside.

## 4 Altar Q
At the base of the stairway in the West Court of the Acropolis is a square monument of enormous archeological importance. Around the four sides of this box-shaped stone are carved portraits of the 16 rulers of Copán. Each is seated on a glyph of his name, which serves as a throne. The monument was dedicated by Copán's last ruler, Yax Pasaj Chan Yopaat (First Dawned Sky Lightening God, 763–c. 810).

## 5 Ball court

Copán's ball court is the most perfect of any Classic-period Mayan site. Macaw head sculptures served as markers, and the doorways, jambs and façades of surrounding temples were ornamented with carved figures of the rain god Chac and other deities. At its north end are at least 63 carved stelae and 14 altar structures. Spectators stood on stepped platforms to watch the ball game.

## 6 Great Plaza

Built by 18 Rabbit, the Great Plaza is filled with monuments in his honour. Stelae depict him in the guise of various deities, such as wearing the jade-decorated costume of the maize god. Other monuments connect him to the Mayan creation myth. The arrangement of monuments on the plaza may be linked to cosmic events, such as the movements of Venus and the constellations.

# The glory of Palenque

*The great city of Palenque, set deep in the jungles of the Mayan highlands close to the Usumacinta River, has become perhaps the single most popular and archetypal Mayan city. This is, in no small part, due to the discoveries made by Alberto Ruz Lhuillier in 1952 (see page 126), when Palenque's Temple of the Inscriptions was discovered to be the final resting place of the Mayan king Pacal the Great, who ruled from 615 to 683 CE.*

*Opposite: The Temple of the Inscriptions has become the single most iconic architectural symbol of Mayan cultural achievement – a lasting tribute to the visionary work of Pacal the Great.*

The fact that his tomb was covered by a mysteriously carved lid, and his face by a beautiful and carefully constructed jade mosaic mask, made the discovery all the more important and intriguing. Pacal suddenly became the Tutankhamun of the Mayan world – and the Temple of the Inscriptions his Great Pyramid. Combined with the wealth of jade artefacts and the ornate reliefs within the tomb chamber, the discovery became the richest of any that had been made on the American continent.

## The Temple of Inscriptions

It was Pacal the Great – or K'inich Janaab' Pakal as he was known to the Maya – who was responsible for most of the great architectural achievements that can still be seen at Palenque. He initiated the Temple of the Inscriptions as his funerary monument, and it subsequently fell to his son K'inich Kan B'ahlam (and possibly his grandson K'inich Akal Mo'Naab') to complete the works following Pacal's death in 683. This stepped pyramid epitomizes Classic-era architectural achievement. On top of its nine-stage stepped platform is the temple of its name. For many years, the main interest in this building was the large panel of hieroglyphics that gives the temple its modern name. It is the second-largest collection of glyphic texts in the world and records some 180 years of Palenque's history. Indeed, one of the most important features of Palenque is that it was the first Mayan city to yield up a list of dynastic rulers.

*Below: Glyphs from the Temple of the Cross at Palenque tell the story of the ancestral rulers of Palenque, some of whom predate the current Mayan age.*

## Other structures

But the Temple of the Inscriptions is not the only important building at Palenque, and structures given names such as the Temple of the Cross, Temple of the Foliated Cross, Temple of the Sun, Temple of the Wind and the Palace have also played a large part in revealing more about the history of Palenque and its ritual practices. But despite the intense focus on Palenque, and its importance in the study of the Maya and their understanding of the world, it is estimated that only 5 per cent of the city has so far been recovered from its jungle hiding place.

As we shall see later, it is through an understanding of Pacal the Great and his role in the Mayan world that predictions about 2012 may reveal a completely new meaning.

# Rediscovering the Maya

*The story of Palenque's re-discovery contains many elements which are typical in the West's wider encounter with the ancient Maya. When Palenque was first encountered in 1773 by a European, Friar Ordoñez – a priest of the nearby town of Ciudad Real – the buildings of the city were completely overgrown. Local native peoples had known about the place for the hundreds of years since its demise, but none had wished to recover it from the ownership of the jungle. When Friar Ordoñez had completed his exploration of the city, his response was a combination of the academic and the speculative.*

*Many people first became aware of the Maya's cultural achievement through the illustrations and etchings of Frederick Catherwood.*

### Ordoñez's story

Ordoñez wrote a monograph about the site entitled *A History of the Creation of Heaven and Earth*. In the book he called Palenque 'The City of Serpents' and attempted to explain its significance in relation to local myths. His story made the claim that the original Palenque had been constructed by a group of people who had come from the Atlantic, led by a man called Votan. Ordoñez had discovered this story in the writings of another priest (a previous Bishop of Chiapas named Nuñes de la Vega), who had copied down part of a Quiché Maya manuscript before burning it in 1691 along with many other Mayan texts.

After Friar Ordoñez's great discovery, Palenque was partially cleared by a captain of artillery, Don Antonio del Rio, who came to the startling conclusion that these ornate buildings were the work of the Romans, or perhaps of other civilizations that had visited the Americas from the old world. It was not until 1839 that a wealthy American lawyer named John Stephens and the English artist and draughtsman Frederick Catherwood embarked on a full-scale exploration of some 44 Mayan sites.

### Stephens' discoveries

Stephens' own impressions of their remarkable discoveries speak of his surprise and humility in the face of an unexpectedly developed civilization. On discovering the lost city of Copán, Stephens wrote:

*Architecture, sculpture, and painting, all the arts which embellish life, had flourished in this overgrown forest; orators, warriors, and statesmen, beauty, ambition, and glory had lived and passed away, and none knew that such things had been, or could tell of their past existence. Books, the records of knowledge, are silent on this theme. The city was desolate. No remnant of this race hangs round the ruins, with traditions handed down from father to son and from generation to generation. It lay before us like a shattered bark in the midst of the ocean, her mast gone, her name effaced, her crew perished, and none to tell whence she came, to whom she belonged, how long on her journey, or what caused her destruction...*

## Decoding the hieroglyphics

What was clear from the monuments, and from some of the few documents that had survived the early Spanish purges, was that the Maya possessed a complex language. Researchers had witnessed the work of Jean-François Champollion in deciphering parts of the Rosetta Stone's hieroglyphics in 1822, and it seemed reasonable that if the Egyptian language could crack under the penetrating study of academics, then the Mayan language would soon fall too. This offered the hope that perhaps the mysteries – not just of the great Mayan civilization, but of its sudden and curious disappearance – might one day be solved. But whereas the Rosetta Stone contained three languages elucidating the same content, which made the decipherer's job much easier, the Mayan texts had no such sources of comparison. The decoding of the Mayan hieroglyphs was to be considerably harder.

In his book *Incidents of Travel in Central America, Chiapas and Yucatán*, Stephens describes his first impression of seeing the achievements of Mayan culture:

*Here were the remains of a cultivated, polished, and peculiar people, who had passed through all the stages incident to the rise and fall of nations; reached their golden age, and perished... We went up to their desolate temples and fallen altars: and wherever we moved we saw the evidence of their taste, their skill in arts... We called back into life the strange people who gazed in sadness from the wall; pictured them, in fanciful costumes and adorned with plumes of feather, ascending the terraces of the palace and the steps leading to the temples... In the romance of the world's history nothing ever impressed me more forcibly than the spectacle of this once great and lovely city, overturned, desolate, and lost... overgrown with trees all around, and without even a name to distinguish it.*

Frederick Catherwood's drawings and engravings were a perfect complement to the writings of Stephens, and the creation of their first book in 1841 and of their second, *Incidents of Travel in Yucatán*, in 1843 were the first to provide European researchers with a full picture of the splendour and gravity of Mayan achievements.

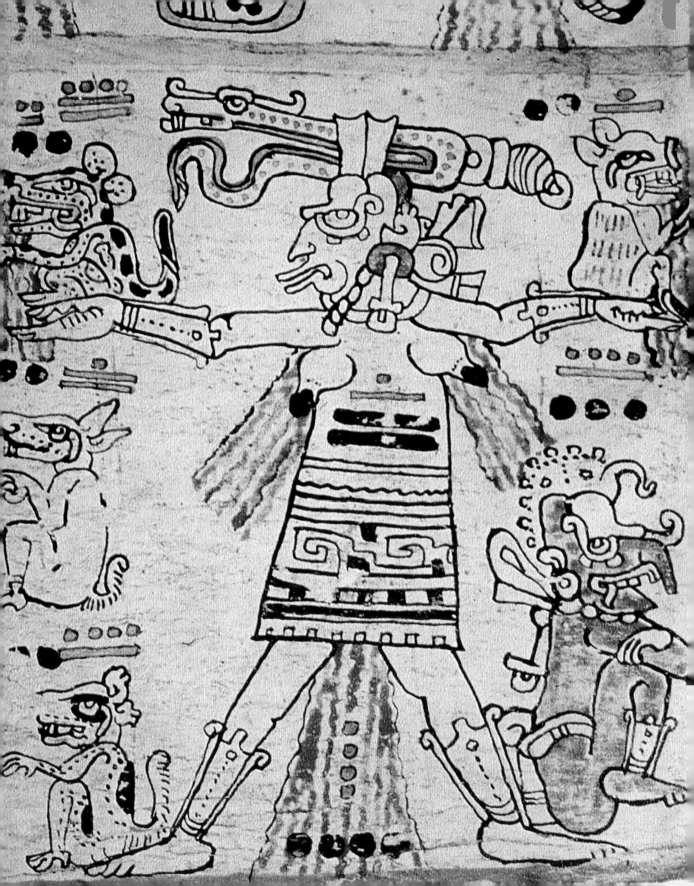

## De Bourbourg's manuscript discoveries

In the late 1840s a Frenchman by the name of Charles Etienne Brasseur de Bourbourg arrived in Mexico wishing to make sense of Meso-American culture. Supported by influential friends, he gained access to the history of the Aztecs, as written down by the Mexican historian Fernando de Alva Cortés Ixtlilxóchitl. He befriended a descendant of one of Montezuma's brothers, who helped teach him the native language of Nahuatl and, travelling widely throughout the region, de Bourbourg rediscovered many manuscripts that had lain unrecognized and gathering dust in various Spanish Catholic libraries. Perhaps the most important of these was a Mayan text called the Popol Vuh. By learning Quiché and Cakchiquel, the two relevant Mayan dialects, de Bourbourg was able to translate the work, which emerged as the greatest written Mayan creation myth.

## The codices

Respected for his finds, de Bourbourg was given access to Bishop Diego de Landa's 16th-century *Rélacion de las Cosas de Yucatán*, with its drawings of Mayan hieroglyphs. By studying this, he was able to start deciphering the symbols. A further leap forward was taken when he met Professor Jean de Tro y Orlano, a descendant of Hernan Cortés, who revealed that his family had been in possession of a Mayan codex. This astonishing document, which became known as the Troano Codex, was made up of 70 pages of hieroglyphic images, drawn in inks and coloured pigments on accordion-folded sheets of limewashed tree bark.

In 1988 another French researcher, Léon de Rosny, found 42 pages of another Mayan codex, known as the Cortesianus Codex. When these were brought together with the Troano, it was discovered that they formed one document. This was named the Tro-Cortesianus Codex, or Madrid Codex. De Rosny would discover the glyphs that denoted the four cardinal points of north, south, east and west. In two of these points was contained the symbol for 'sun', *kin*, which also means day in the Mayan calendar. Modern decoding was under way.

Another two codices were discovered, or rediscovered, in the 18th and 19th centuries. Perhaps the most important, detailed and elaborate of all is the Dresden Codex, bought by the royal library of the court of Saxony in Dresden in 1739, but only seriously studied from 1867 when Ernst Förstemann made facsimiles and began its decoding. Analysing the glyphs, he uncovered the symbols for the moon and for the Mayan 20-day month known as the *uinal* (pronounced 'weenal'). He deciphered the glyph for 'beginning' – a head image called *akbal* – and for 'end'. *Akbal* also means night and represents the start of the Mayan month.

## The Venus calendar

Förstemann was also to discover astronomical information: the Eclipse Data, which told Mayan priests when lunar and solar eclipses would occur, and, perhaps more importantly, the Venus calendar, a set of long and detailed tables occupying five pages of the codex, which charted the average length of the cycle of the planet Venus over many years. It also identified what the Maya called the birth date of Venus on 13 August 3114 BCE in our Gregorian calendar – the beginning of the current era that is due to end in 2012.

These breakthroughs have enabled later scholars to make progress in decoding the monuments and codices that still exist – and still prove elusive and enigmatic. Even today, new advances in our understanding of the Maya are rewriting their history and giving us a more truthful picture of their world and their vision.

*The Madrid Codex, with its colourful images of gods, animals and animal-human hybrids, is composed of almanacs based on the 260-day Tzolkin calendar.*

# The demise of the Maya

*What other means have been used to find out about the culture and lives of the Maya people? And how have these shed light on the rise and fall of Mayan civilization? In his book* Collapse, *Jared Diamond has examined the various theories and evidence that exist to explain the sudden disappearances of Maya populations at the seeming peak of their prosperity and cultural development – most of which occurred around the period between 700 and 1000.*

Drawing on various kinds of archeological data, Diamond concluded that the collapse of the Classic Maya was the result of a number of factors – any of which could have been decisive, but together were conclusive.

### Deforestation and climate change

The first factor was the very success of Mayan civilization. With the technical ability to grow food in large quantities, there was the potential to support equally large populations. At the same time, however, the soil that had grown last year's crop could not necessarily sustain next year's crop. And when city societies started to 'slash and burn' the forest, expanding their 'fields' to grow more maize, they began to reach the limits of their success. Deforestation of hillsides – to make way for agriculture and provide the raw materials for large building projects – cannot go on indefinitely. There are consequences that modern humans are also aware of. One of the first effects of large-scale deforestation is localized climate change. Without tree cover, rainfall is less dependable and drought becomes more likely. There is also the problem of soil erosion and the dangers of landslips engulfing large areas of human habitation.

Examination by scientists of some of the larger lakes in the Mayan region has yielded important information. By drilling sediment cores from the bottoms of lakes and applying radiocarbon dating to their finds, it has been possible for archeologists to determine times when there was more or less rainfall. Sediments from drier times contain higher proportions of Oxygen-18, a rarer isotope of oxygen than 'normal' Oxygen-16. From their findings they maintain that the Mayan region was generally wet from 5500 BCE (well before the start of the current Long Count era) until 500 BCE. From 475 BCE to 250 BCE it was drier, but became wetter again until around 125 CE, when a drought began that appears to have lasted until 250 CE. During this Pre-Classic period, archeologists maintain that there was a 'collapse' of population at the Mayan city known to us as El Mirador.

### Years of drought and decline

From 250 onwards, wetter conditions again held sway until a drought in around 600 coincided with decline at the great city of Tikal. In about 760 the worst droughts for some

*Many theories have been proposed to explain how such impressive architectural achievements as Tikal could have simply been left to the mercy of the jungle.*

*Chichén Itzá in the Yucatán continued to be occupied beyond the Classic Maya era that saw the end of other major cities. This period saw the dominance of other peoples, such as the Itzas, who superseded the Maya.*

7,000 years started: two dry years around 760 itself; a dry decade between 810 and 820; three dry years around 860; and six dry years around 910. Interestingly, these coincide with some of the major collapses in the Mayan city-states. Perhaps even more significant is the theory that they closely match the cycle of the 52-year Calendar Round, and that modern climatologists acknowledge the reality of the 208-year (four x 52) drought cycle resulting from corresponding cycles of solar radiation.

## Inter-civic strife

We must also be aware of the effects of conflicts between city-states – conflicts that may themselves have been exacerbated by climate factors. Until recently there was an image of the Maya people as the peace-loving hippies of the first millennium. While they were advanced, both culturally and spiritually, the truth is that they did not lead violence-free lives. And as competition for resources in the Mayan region grew with the increasing population, so did the number of conflicts between the priest-kings whose role it was to protect the interests of their people. There is evidence that these inter-civic wars, along with the resource problems they caused, may have led to widespread death and devastation. Alongside the possibility of long periods of drought, there may have been little hope for the sustainability of Mayan culture.

## The decline of Copán

The history of Copán provides an interesting example of the way in which the Maya saw their civilization rise and fall, a cycle that was, in some way, an inevitable result of their evolutionary cycle – and one to which we, as resource managers in the modern day, might do well to pay attention.

Copán, in what is now western Honduras, was a small but densely built city in a river valley surrounded by steep hills (see page 36). Its first Long Count inscription was made in 426 CE, when nobles or attackers arrived from Tikal and Teotihuacán and seem to have absorbed Copán into their empire. This influx led to the building of huge royal monuments around 650. Not content to reserve these honours for kings, the lower levels of nobles and aristocracy decided it was their turn. By 700 palaces for the nobles were under way and by 800 about 20 had been built. One of these palaces was made up of 50 buildings and would have housed about 250 people. And who would have supported this lavish lifestyle? The peasants, of course. And so the pressure to produce food and provide luxury goods, such as jade, shells and feathers, fell on the lower ranks.

Although Copán's main agricultural growing area was in the fertile river-valley bottom, increased demands started to drive agriculture (and farmers' lives and homes) up the hillsides from 650 onwards. But this move had its limits: although at one point 40 per cent of farming was being carried out on the hillsides, archeology has revealed that the valley floor became filled with sediment from the hills during the 8th century.

The push to get more from the deforested, acidic land had not worked. Indeed, the good soils in the valley were now contaminated with the poorer soils running down the hills. Analysis of human skeletons recovered from the Copán sites, and tested for stress lines in teeth and porous bones, has revealed that malnutrition and other resultant diseases increased between 650 and 850. And although this was affecting the entire population, it was, predictably, the peasants who took the brunt of the failing resources.

The last large buildings at Copán were erected around 800, and the last Long Count date was inscribed into an altar honouring a king (and never completed) in 822.

## The collapse of Mayan civilization

Analysis at other sites throughout the Mayan region has shown that some cities were still booming as late as 900 or 925, but then suffered collapse within another 50 years. Chichén Itzá, perhaps the largest city on the northern part of the Yucatán peninsula, continued to grow after 1000 and only fell as a result of civil war in around 1250. Altogether, though, it is estimated that destruction and death brought an end to between 90 and 99 per cent of all Maya peoples after 800. Beyond that time everything that could have been called civilization, including the Long Count calendar and the rituals of Mayan spiritual life, was to disappear from view, never to return.

Whether the Maya would have considered their own rise and fall an inevitable cycle is a difficult question to answer. Perhaps, though, in the microcosm of their Classic civilization we might be able to see our own society reflected. We have lived with an image of untrammelled growth and continuous technological development for many hundreds of years. We have believed that it has no end – merely constant improvement, increased luxury and easier lives. Perhaps the truth we are now beginning to recognize is a similar reality to that faced by the Maya: that constant expansion has its limits; that we are also subject to natural forces; and that the cycles of nature may be more powerful than our ability to subjugate the natural world to our whims.

*All forms of civilization at Copán disappeared beneath the jungle following the city's demise. In the modern age the artistry of Copán's craftsmen has been uncovered and restored.*

# Chapter 3

# THE MAYAN WORLD VIEW

When the first Spanish conquistadores arrived in the Yucatán peninsula, the Maya – along with their Aztec counterparts further west – were viewed as demonic worshippers of Satan by the Catholic aggressors. And yet, over the last four hundred years, the Maya have gradually been rehabilitated. They have now rightly come to be respected as probably the greatest culture that ever existed on the American continent.

For the Maya, everything they created had a relationship to their understanding of the universe and the order that lay behind it. Their spirituality, culture and art were all true reflections of their world view. As masters of time and prophecy, they sought to express this through every possible avenue, be this religious ritual and practice, artistic expression and production, or literary achievement. Consistent themes emerge: cycles of time, ritual and death, the destructive forces of nature and, perhaps overriding all of these, a fascination with the movements of the stars above.

# Mayan deities

*In looking at the concepts and rituals of the Maya, it is important to distinguish between the many manifestations of different Mayan groupings. In the 16th century, when the Maya were first encountered by European peoples, there were around 30 distinct Mayan languages, most of which can still be found across Meso-America today.*

*This terracotta urn represents the Maya's one supreme deity Itzam Ná, the original creator of hieroglyphic writing.*

## Mayan differences and similarities

There were also contrasts and differences between the Maya of the northern, Yucatán lowlands and the highland people of Chiapas, southern Guatemala and Honduras, who had individual tribal names such as Chorti, Kekchi, Quiché, Mam, Tzotzil and Tojolabal. Religious and calendrical observances such as the Long Count (see page 84), which were important to the Maya people of the Yucatán peninsula, were, by the 16th century, considerably less important to the Post-Classic peoples of the highlands.

In some cases, however, the concepts and rituals that were important to one group were also significant to many other groups, but were given a different name. Quetzalcoatl, or the Plumed Serpent of central South America, was known in the Yucatán as Kukulkán and in the highland areas of the Quiché and Cakchiquel peoples as Gucumatz (see pages 53 and 120).

## The pantheon of Mayan gods

As with many cultures, the Maya believed there was a creation time during which the gods set the pattern for human life. The gods themselves were born, grew, underwent rites of passage and initiations, experienced transformations, died and were reborn, often being elevated to a greater status and perhaps even as celestial objects. In Mayan mythology the early gods created cornfields where they planted maize, oversaw its growth and then harvested it – the earliest metaphor for the way in which the gods saw human life from their divine perspective. The world was described as a maize field in which people were the maize, grown ready for harvest by the death god, Hun Nal. The deities also carried out divination for prophecies, engaged in wars, created alliances and intermarriages.

The pantheon of Mayan gods was a map for human interaction and provided the model for human conduct among the Mayan elite. Each deity could adopt many different guises, which makes identifying gods a complex process. Although there were around 165 main deities, some Mayan sources put forward the idea of one supreme deity called Itzam Ná (Iguana House) or Ah Xoc Kin, the creator of hieroglyphic writing as well as the patron of arts and sciences. In the daytime he was also the sun god K'inich Ahau, while at night-time the Maya hypothesized that he transformed himself into a jaguar for his nightly sojourn through the underworld. In his feathered-serpent persona, he was also known as Kukulkán, the same Christ-like god presence known to the Aztecs as Quetzalcoatl. Ruling alongside him was Ix'Chel, the goddess of weaving, healing and childbirth.

Chac was one of the most important deities from Meso-American culture and was the source of all rain and lightning. Known to the Aztecs as Tlaloc, he was usually seen wielding axes and serpents as weapons that represented his natural forces. And the ancient Mayan god of death, usually portrayed in skeletal form, was called Yum Cimih, although he was also known as Cizin, or 'the flatulent one'.

## Calendrical deities

Deities were also embedded in the Mayan calendar system. The Classic Maya believed that each division within their calendrical system was ruled by a different deity or set of deities. The day, the night, the solar Haab' year of 365 days, the *katun* of 7,200 days, the lunar cycle and the Venus cycle all had their overlighting gods. Instead of the European perception of Venus as a goddess of love, to the Maya the planet was a heavy male presence – known as Lahun Chan – brooding over the fate of humankind and foreshadowing dark and dangerous events such as wars. When Venus was in the skies, shutters on the windows would be closed. In a way this sounds more like the European interpretation of Mars, a planet the Maya also tracked, but which played a less important role.

These and other gods played significant roles in the spectacularly epic tale of the Popol Vuh (see page 60), in which the people of the world are born to become sustenance for the gods. As we shall see, this image of sacrifice plays an important part in the Mayan calendar and in the Mayan's sense of ultimate destiny for humankind.

## Deities and the cycle of life

The Maya were intimately aware of the deities that ruled any time period, and of how their influence might help or hinder them in their activities. The calendar deities were, however, much more powerful than simply an aspect of divination for auspicious times; they were vital in the ordering and constant renewing of the world that the Mayan cycles of life demanded.

In Mayan rituals, the nobles and rulers would often wear costumes and masks of the gods, taking on their qualities and abilities, and even being perceived by their followers as becoming that god and expressing that god's will (if only temporarily) in their efforts to maintain order in the universe.

*A stela from Santa Lucia Cotzumalguapa in Guatemala depicts a planetary deity and records an astronomical event together with its date.*

Mayan art also tells us much about the relationship between deities and humans. Objects were often involved in rituals and became more valued as a result. Decoration frequently incorporated narrative elements from myth, and glyphs (graphic symbols) telling stories and giving important dates of events. Portrayals of the gods, astronomical symbols and prophetic elements all played their part in what were essentially 'encoded' pieces of art.

Much of this work was commissioned by the high rulers of city-states to adorn their palaces, and to prove to all who witnessed their abundance and taste that they were not just fit to rule, but were intimately linked to the work of the gods. In some cases the works went into their owners' tombs, where their function was to accompany the ruler on his journey to the heavens. Cups and vases showing scenes from court life, and clay figurines portraying many of the characters in a royal personage's life, can all be found; priests, musicians, servants, ball-players, hunchbacks and beautifully coiffured women continued to play their part through their representations.

*The serpent god Kukulkán is represented in this relief sculpture found at the Nunnery at Uxmal, weaving its way across a geometrical background.*

## Deities and the cardinal directions

The gods could make themselves manifest in a number of different guises (as well as through their human rulers), depending on their personal spheres of influence and responsibility. Some might take the forms of natural phenomena, such as lightning and thunder, wind, rain and fire. Others would embody themselves as plants or animals. In the animal domain there were four types of animals: the Crawlers, such as lizards, snakes and turtles; the Walkers, which were predominantly mammals; the Flyers, which included birds and bats as well as flying insects; and the Swimmers, which were the crocodiles, cayman and fish. This fourfold embodiment is familiar throughout Mayan cosmology, with the deities often acting as different forms according to the four different aspects of the cardinal directions – directions that speak of the space and time of the Mayan world.

In fact, the concept of the four primary compass directions is one of the key principles of Mayan belief and integrates their art, architecture and religion. Each direction was associated with particular meanings and significance, and each was represented by a particular colour: north was linked with the colour white, south with yellow, east with red and west with black.

*Mayan vases often portray scenes of ritual life. This one shows the ruler seated on a jaguar throne, taking part in a divinatory ritual with a priest.*

## The story of Kukulkán/Quetzalcoatl

Kukulkán to the Maya, Quetzalcoatl to the Aztecs, is one of the most important gods in Meso-American civilizations. According to Aztec mythology, he was one of the four creator gods – Red Tezcatlipoca or Xipe Totec was associated with the east, Blue Tezcatlipoca or Huitzilopochtli with the south, Black Tezcatlipoca with the north and Quetzalcoatl or White Tezcatlipoca with the west. The struggles and confrontations for supremacy between these four gods led to the creation and destruction of four successive ages or suns.

For the Aztecs, Quetzalcoatl was god of the wind and came to sweep a path for rain. In this form he was a breath of life, which made the vegetation of the Earth sway like a serpent covered in green feathers. He was also held to have been a divine king who brought blessings to the Earth, improved agriculture, was a patron of the arts and taught an enlightened philosophy of gentleness and asceticism (see page 120).

# The underworld and the world tree

*The Maya saw the world as consisting of three levels: the underworld (Xibalbá), which itself consisted of nine layers; the middle world, which was the world of humans; and a heavenly world supported by four gods called the Bakabs. Following the theme of the four directions in Mayan belief (see page 53), the Bakabs were four brothers who held up the sky, one at each cardinal point, each associated with one of the four colours and assigned to a part of the calendar.*

### The underworld

Xibalbá was the place of all fears, the underworld, hell. It was ruled by two gods: Hun Came (One Death) and Vucub Came (Seven Death), who – in the Popol Vuh myth of the Quiché Maya people (see page 60) – were responsible for the deaths of Hun Hunahpú and Vucub Hunahpú, the father and uncle of the Hero Twins. Hun Came and Vucub Came are not alone in Xibalbá: they preside over a whole gang of death gods, who were named by the ways in which they carried out their executions.

In the Popol Vuh, the gods of Xibalbá enforce the tests and challenges of six houses: the House of Bats, the House of Knives, the House of Gloom, the House of Jaguars, the House of Fire and the House of Cold, each one of which offers a more dangerous and fearful experience to the Hero Twins. And just as in the purgatorial models of other religions, the rulers of the Maya (these experiences seem to have been reserved to some extent for the aristocracy) must undergo the tests if they are to be resurrected as celestial objects. Just to reinforce the power of Xibalbá in the psyche of the Maya, it is the death god Bolon Yookte' K'uh who will claim this world for Xibalbá at the end of the fifth Mayan age on 21 December 2012, when according to the predictions of some experts we may all have to experience the trials of Xibalbá.

### The world tree

The world tree was one of the Maya's most powerful images of creation. Originally it was believed that this image was simply a metaphor for the relationship between the three levels of existence (heaven, earth and the underworld): the tree sits on the earth, and its trunk and branches reach towards heaven, while its roots seek the underworld known as Xibalbá. In the Temple of the Cross at Palenque can be see the Wakah Chan, or Raised-up Sky, which portrays this relationship. On the top of the image is Itzam-Yeh, the great bird, with its head in the heavens. At the foot of the image is a water monster, its mouth representing the gateway to Xibalbá.

There are some Mayan scholars who equate the raising of the world tree with actual celestial events occurring at the start of the Mayan Long Count calendar on 13 August 3114 BCE. Linda Schele, the prominent Mayanist and author of *Maya Cosmology*, believes that the world tree raised in Mayan cosmology actually refers to the Milky Way. She came to this conclusion by studying the positions of the stars as they would have been in mid-August 3114 and discovering that the Milky Way would have been running north–south overhead – a veritable axis of the heavens.

The image on the tomb lid of Pacal the Great that was discovered beneath Palenque's Temple of the Inscriptions (see page 130) is also believed by some to portray the Mayan ruler on the world tree, possibly falling into the underworld prior to a heavenly resurrection.

The world tree represents how humans stand between the heavens above and the underworld below them. In an important way, humans mediate between the 13 heavens and the nine hells of Mayan cosmology. The great world tree was the means by which the supernatural world and the natural world could communicate with each other.

*Associated with the setting of the sun, the falling god appears in painted and sculptured imagery such as this ceremonial urn. He is also linked to the maize cult and holds flowers in one hand.*

# Ritual and sacrifice

*One of the most important rituals in religious practice was bloodletting. This painful exercise was carried out by members of the ruling classes as an offering to the gods. Kings and queens would perform bloodletting at every crucial stage of their lives and at significant completion times in the calendar's cycles.*

*Opposite: A lintel from Temple 23 at Yaxchilan shows the ruler Jewel Jaguar watching his wife Lady Xoc perform a bloodletting ritual by passing a rope embedded with thorns through her tongue.*

*Below: Stela A at Copán in Honduras portrays the famous ruler 18 Rabbit surrounded by solar creatures and symbols of the bloodletting rituals.*

## The practice of bloodletting

Bloodletting involved piercing to release blood, which was collected on special paper. The most significant body parts for male rulers were the ear, tongue and foreskin. From the excavation of burial sites, it has been revealed that women rulers pierced in their genital region as well. The rite was performed with sharpened bone or spines from the manta ray.

Once the blood had been collected, the stained paper was burned in a ritual fire to honour the gods and ask for their power in maintaining the order of the cosmos and continuity of life. There may have been political aspects to the ritual, as it could be seen as way for rulers to reinforce their own importance in the divine creative process. This worked so long as the crops continued to grow and their city-states flourished. However, as rulers found their kingdoms disintegrating, they are recorded as travelling from one city to another performing bloodletting rituals, in order to prevent chaos overrunning them.

It is believed priests would administer hallucinogens to the rulers prior to the painful bloodletting, as a painkiller and a means of closer communion between the ruler and his gods. Drugs such as Bal'Ché – made from tree bark and honey, wild tobacco, the seeds of certain plants and some mushrooms – were certainly used by the Maya at different times. In addition to the rulers ingesting psychoactive drugs orally, figurines suggest that some drugs were ingested anally as an enema, because this was thought (correctly) to help the substances enter the bloodstream more quickly and give a more powerful 'hit'. Perhaps the strangest form of psychoactive drug was the tropical giant toad (*Bufo marinus*), whose skin exudations, when ingested, were a powerful aid to achieving altered mental states.

## Human sacrifice

For a long time the Maya were thought to be peace-loving, non-violent people, living an idyllic hippy-like life in the jungle. They were contrasted with the bloodthirsty Aztecs, who could carry out tens (or even hundreds) of thousands of human sacrifices each year. But as the understanding of hieroglyphics increased, it became clear that conflict and bloodshed were as much a part of Mayan life as they were of Aztec. Just as the bloodletting rituals of the rulers were supposed to nourish and propitiate the gods, so could the sacrifice of prisoners, slaves and, particularly, children. Indeed, it is now thought that orphans and illegitimate children were bought specially for occasions of ritual sacrifice.

The Maya believed death from natural causes was undesirable, since it did not guarantee a journey to the upper worlds. Sacrifice, however, pleased the gods and could guarantee a place in the heavens. A good death, the Maya believed, was as important as a good life.

# Mystical revelations from art

*Since the almost simultaneous discovery of murals at the Mayan site of Bonampak, close to Palenque, in 1946 by two separate Americans – conscientious objector Carlos Frey and explorer Giles Healey – a great deal of focus has fallen on what have been the most important Mayan paintings to have been recovered from the obscurity of the Meso-American jungles. These murals offer an incredible insight into Mayan myth and ritual, and in particular into the importance of bloodletting.*

*The murals at Bonampak were originally rendered in very bright colours, but have suffered from careless restoration work. Their 20th-century discoverers threw kerosene on the paintings in the hope of improving them.*

Professor Mary Miller of Yale University has said, 'Perhaps no single artefact from the ancient New World offers as complex a view of pre-Hispanic society as do the Bonampak paintings. No other work features so many Maya engaged in the life of the court and rendered in such great detail, making the Bonampak murals an unparalleled resource for understanding ancient society.'

## The Bonampak murals

The paintings at Bonampak have been shown to date from 790 and were made as frescoes in fresh plaster in a limited number of short sessions. The murals are contained within three rooms and appear to show a series of historical events rendered in a realistic style.

The first room shows priests and nobles being robed in preparation for a ceremony. The murals continue with an image of the ceremony itself, in which a child appears to be confirmed as heir to a noble dynasty. An orchestra plays drums, wooden trumpets and other musical instruments. One of

the musicians wears crab-like claws, while nobles confer together. The second room portrays a scene of war, and continues with the Lords of Bonampak taking prisoners (shown with bleeding fingers), apparently for human sacrifice. The action of the paintings in room three takes place in front of a pyramid and depicts a further ceremony involving the Lords of Bonampak. Here they are shown piercing their tongues in a ritual act of bloodletting. There are also hieroglyphics that give Long Count dates for the events and names of the major characters taking part.

As well as confirming Mayan expertise in large paintings, the murals have been analysed by some experts for coded content. Maurice Cotterell, in his book *The Supergods*, argues that the image showing musicians in the first room contains hidden information revealing a quite different story. He maintains that his unusual visual analysis of the imagery shows a whole separate narrative about Xipe Totec, the god of the east, and of flaying and bloody sacrifice.

## San Bartolo

In 2003 a stunning set of murals were discovered at San Bartolo in northern Guatemala, northeast of Tikal. Beneath a 25-metre (85-foot) pyramid known as Las Ventanas (The Windows), archeologists from the Harvard team excavating San Bartolo were amazed to find a room covered with 12 metres (40 feet) of paintings showing elaborate mythological scenes. The room, now known as the Cuarto de las Pinturas (The Room of the Paintings) has been described by the head of the Harvard team as the Mayan equivalent of the Vatican's Sistine Chapel.

Radiocarbon dating of the mural at around 250 BCE has confirmed important new aspects of Mayan culture and mythology. Here is evidence that the most significant of the Mayan creation myths – the Popol Vuh – was part of Mayan culture more than 2,000 years ago. A large bicephalus (two-headed) bird sits in the top of a tree, a representation of Vucub Caquix, who was killed by the Hero Twins of the Popol Vuh, which had until then only been known as a text of the Quiché Maya people, first written in around 1550. And so it is to a deeper examination of the Popol Vuh that we now need to turn.

*This 'rollout' of a vase's exterior decoration shows the typical polychromatic decoration of the Chama-style vase, with its chevron borders. Originally from the Chama area in Guatemala, the style spread during the Maya Classic period.*

# The Popol Vuh: the key Mayan myth

*The Popol Vuh, which was rediscovered and translated by Charles Etienne Brasseur de Bourbourg, reveals the central creation myth of the Quiché Maya, although it is possible that other Mayan tribes had their own versions of the myth. Even though the manuscript was produced in the 16th century CE, the Popol Vuh contains many of the characters and events known from other sources to have been present in the mythology of the Classic Maya at least 700 years before.*

*From a panel found at Toniná, this glyph represents the ancient Mayan ball-game. Toniná, like many Mayan sites, had its own ball-court.*

Much of the evidence for the antiquity of the Popol Vuh comes from Mayan art. The paintings of San Bartolo, dated to 250 BCE, reveal key elements of the myth (see page 59). Another important piece of evidence comes in the form of the Princeton Vase, which, according to some scholars, is the finest example of Mayan art.

The vase shows the underworld God L and the Hero Twins in a setting that resembles a royal court or palace. In the intricately depicted scene, God L is tying a jade bracelet

around the wrist of a young woman, while the Hero Twins – both masked to hide their identities – are apparently performing a magic trick. In the background one court attendant seems to be frothing chocolate by pouring it from one vase to another.

The line rendering of the characters is particularly subtle. The vase is believed to have been created between 600 and 800, and was discovered at Nakbé in the northern Petén area of present-day Guatemala. In portraying a scene from the Popol Vuh, the vase reinforces the myth's central importance in the everyday belief system of the Maya.

## The ball-game in the Popol Vuh

The Popol Vuh reveals many of the central preoccupations of the Maya. Here we see cycles of time, worlds coming to cataclysmic ends, the extraordinary power of nature and the integration of deities into the starry world above. However, one key element of the Popol Vuh needs further explanation before the myth can be fully appreciated – the famous ball-game played throughout Meso-America, which the gods in the Popol Vuh play too.

While 21st-century culture is 'football crazy', the Classic Maya and the cultures that preceded them were obsessed with the ball-game.

*This Late Classic-era relief depicts a figure wearing the protective and ritualistic costume of the ball-player. Great players and important games were sometimes celebrated in carved stone panels.*

All the major city-states of the Mayan lands contained a ball-court. They were not identical in shape and structure, but the most popular configuration was an I-shape, with two sloping sides that (it is presumed) provided greater challenge within the action of the game. Players in this often violent game wore special protection for their arms and legs.

Most of the ball-courts had a ring, or series of rings, embedded vertically in one of the walls. As in basketball, teams would aim to pass the ball – which could be any size, from tennis-ball to football size – through this ring in order to score. There has been great speculation about the fate of the losing team in any game, and many experts believe that death was the penalty for failure – a theme that seems to concur with the mythological origins of the game and its appearance in the Popol Vuh.

## The creation story of Popul Vuh

The Popol Vuh begins in stillness and peace before the world exists, when only a vague sea is pooled under the sky. Then Gucumatz, the Plumed Serpent God, and Huracan, the Heart of Heaven, create the landscape and the animals out of their words. But the languageless animals cannot praise their gods and are condemned to become food for speaking people, who are yet to be born. At first the two gods attempt to create these humans from clay, but they are too fragile and soon return to dirt.

The great gods ask for help from an old seer couple, Xpiyacoc and Xmucane, who – while they count the days of the sacred Tzolkin calendar – determine that humans should be made from wood. Immediately the world is filled with men made of wood and women made from reeds. Although they can speak, these figures are without souls and still unable to praise their gods and so must be destroyed; a flood comes, a rain of resin falls from the sky and demons arrive to pull the wooden people apart. The only surviving descendants are turned into forest monkeys and allowed to live on, as a warning of the wooden people's failure. As the first part of the Popol Vuh comes to a close, the gods are still in need of humans who can worship them with prayers and offerings.

## The journey of the twins

The first twins are the children of the seers Xpiyacoc and Xmucane and are known by their names in the sacred Tzolkin calendar: Hun Hunahpú (One Hunahpú) and Vucub Hunahpú (Seven Hunahpú). They grow up to be lovers of the great ball-game, and the court where they play is actually the route to the underworld called Xibalbá.

When the lords of the underworld, Hun Came (One Death) and Vucub Came (Seven Death), hear the thunderous din of the ball-game above them, they decide to kill the twins by tricking them to follow four owl messengers sent from the underworld. The twins take the long and dangerous journey through rapids, past spiky thorns and across a river of blood. They manage to negotiate these and other tests, but a final humiliating challenge requires them to keep cigars and torches alight all through the night, while enclosed in the House of Gloom.

In the morning the gods discover the twins have failed: they are ritually killed and buried in Xibalbá's own ball-court, except for Hun Hunahpú's head, which is placed in a dead-looking tree. Immediately the tree is filled with ripe gourds – one of which is Hun Hunahpú's head. A young woman of the underworld named Xquic passes the tree and, when she stretches out her hand to pick a fruit, Hun Hunahpú's head spits in her palm. This causes Xquic to conceive a child.

Xquic's father, one of the underworld gods, discovers that his daughter is pregnant and decides he will have to kill her. But, with the help of messenger owls, she escapes to the upper world of the Earth, where she finds her way to Xmucane, mother of the two dead twins, and tells her that she is Hun Hunahpú's wife. Soon Xquic gives birth to the true Hero Twins of the Popol Vuh: Hunahpú and Xbalanque.

*Above: Evidence for the barbarity of the ball-game, this Late Classic clay figure shows a successful player holding the skull of a defeated enemy as a trophy in his left hand.*

*Opposite: Mythical aspects of the ball-game were often recorded on the typical Maya Classic-period polychromatic cylinder vases.*

### The attack of Seven Macaw

Soon a flood comes, bringing terrible monsters to live on the surface of the Earth. The worst of these is Vucub Caquix (Seven Macaw), the vainest of all creatures, who declares himself to be the sun and the moon, the lord of the universe. The Hero Twins decide to kill the bird and, when he lands in his favourite fruit tree, Hunahpú shoots him in the head with his blowpipe. The attack is not fatal and the wild and furious Vucub Caquix rips off Hunahpú's arm and flies away with it. But, with the help of an elderly couple who are healers and magicians, the twins trick Vucub Caquix into surrendering his eyes and teeth. The powerless bird no longer has a reason for any vanity and quickly dies, before the old healers place Hunahpú's arm back on its stump, restoring the twin to his full strength.

### The tests of the Hero Twins

Like their father and uncle, the Hero Twins learn to play the ball-game in the ball-court. Again the lords of Xibalbá are disturbed by the terrible noise of their play, and the cycle of conflict between the twins and the gods begins again. This time, however, the outcome is to be different. Threatened by the arrival of the twins, the gods set them the same impossible test: they are given cigars and torches and incarcerated in the House of Gloom for the

*Built during the period of Zapotec culture, the Ball Court at Monte Alban, Oaxaca, was used for a version of the game called* lachi, *in which the aim was to get the ball into the opponents' end of the I-shaped court.*

night. Unlike their ancestors, the new twins attach coloured feathers to the torches to make them appear lit, and place fireflies on the cigars so that they seem to burn. In the morning the victorious twins challenge the gods and claim the right to life.

But the next day the gods present Hunahpú and Xbalanque with a new set of tests for the following night. After successfully negotiating the House of Knives, the House of Cold, the House of Jaguars and the House of Fire, they are invited into the House of Bats. The twins manage to hide inside their own blowpipe guns, but Hunahpú makes a fatal mistake when he looks out to see if the sun is rising – and Camazotz, the killer bat god, swiftly cuts off his head.

## Death and rebirth

The death gods take Hunahpú's head to the ball-court, where they all rejoice at their victory over the twins. But the war is not over. Just before dawn Xbalanque calls on the animals to bring their food, and a coati – a racoon-like animal – brings a large squash, which Xbalanque places on Hunahpú's lifeless body. The squash is transformed into a new head and Hunahpú is able to see and speak and hear again. As dawn breaks, the twins suddenly appear in the underworld ball-court ready for a final confrontation with the gods.

*The stone rings visible at Mayan ball-courts were used as the target for the ball, much like the hoops on a basketball court of today.*

The gods throw Hunahpú's head into the arena to serve as the ball, but Xbalanque hits the head with such force that it ends up in the woods. In the confusion, Xbalanque manages to retrieve the head and place it back on his brother's body, making him whole again. Stung by their loss in the ball-court, the death gods build a pit of fire and encourage the Hero Twins to jump over it. The twins decide that they will make the sacrifice that is demanded: they jump into the flames and are burned to death.

To make absolutely sure of their victory, the death gods grind the dead twins' bones to dust and throw it into the river. Instead of being dispersed, however, the dust of the twins' bones settles on the river bed, and five days later the twins are reborn as fish-men.

## The Hero Twins triumph

The following day the twins return to Xibalbá, disguised as poor wandering performers. They perform many dances, impressing the gods, but this is not enough. The gods command them to kill a dog and bring it back to life. The twins carry out the sacrifice and resurrect the dog. The gods then command them to kill a man and bring him back to to life. Again, the twins carry out the sacrifice and bring the man back to life.

The two chief death gods, Hun Came and Vucub Came, cannot contain their excitement at the performers' feats of magic. They order the twins to kill them and bring them back to life. The twins kill just one of the gods, but leave his body unrestored and unresurrected. His companion, realizing he has been outwitted, begs for pity. His supporters turn away from him, make their way to a canyon and throw themselves to their deaths.

The Hero Twins reveal their true identities to all the surviving Xibalbáns, who beg for mercy and humbly show them the remains of their father Hun Hunahpú and their uncle Vucub Hunahpú, whom the twins then resurrect. The Hero Twins have beaten the gods of death and overcome the evils of Xibalbá; nevermore will Xibalbá hold sway over the lives of human beings. Having made peace with their ancestors, Xbalanque and Hunahpú are raised up into the heavens, where they become the sun and the moon.

## The Books of Chilam Balam

As we can see from the appearance of its narrative in so many art forms, the Popol Vuh was central to the ideas in Mayan culture about life, death and the hope of defeating the destructive forces of the universe. The other key surviving literary sources of myth and prophecy for the Maya are the Books of Chilam Balam, a collection of mythological texts that are identified by the Yucatán towns where they originated: Chumayel, Mani and Tizimin. Originally these books were credited to a legendary oracular priest named Balam and they include many predictions, including that of the arrival of the Spanish conquistadores to the Yucatán peninsula.

The Books of Chilam Balam are generally dated to the 18th and 19th centuries, although they refer to myths, history, medicine and calendrical and astrological predictions from much further back in time. Written in the language of the Yucatec Maya, they are transcribed into European script. Even so, they have proved relatively difficult to translate. Where they have been translated, they have revealed much about the link between Mayan mythology and the sacred calendar.

The three Chilam Balam narratives from Chumayel, Mani and Tizimin contain almost identical references to a flood and a subsequent world resurrection. These can be understood as the starting point of the current Mayan world and are identified with an event in which five trees are established – one at each corner of the world, as well as a central tree – to hold up the sky. The Chumayel book describes the event in detail:

*The Books of Chilam Balam were designed to protect and encode the hidden knowledge of the Yucatec Maya. This page comes from an 18th-century edition created in Ixil in the Yucatán.*

*After the destruction of the world was completed, they placed a tree to set up in its order the yellow cock oriole. Then the white tree of abundance was set up. A pillar of the sky was set up, a sign of the destruction of the world; that was the white tree of abundance in the north. Then the black tree of abundance was set up in the west for the black-breasted 'pidzoy' to sit upon. Then the yellow tree of abundance was set up in the south, as a symbol of the destruction of the world, for the yellow-breasted 'pidzoy' to sit upon, for the yellow cock oriole to sit upon, the timid 'mut'. Then the green tree of abundance was set up in the centre of the world as a record of the destruction of the world.*

*The Mural of the Four Suns, created around 800 at Toniná, portrays the four eras of human history. At the centre of each panel, blood pours from the decapitated head of a prisoner, forming a ring of feathers that also represents the sun.*

In the world of the Maya, the spectre of previous destructions was always present, an everlasting reminder that it was the gods who had the final say over human life. For the conflagrations of the past could also be the apocalypse of the future, as the cycles of life and the heavens played out their inevitable fate.

# Chapter 4

# THE MAYAN CALENDAR IN DEPTH

The Mayan Long Count calendar is perhaps the greatest legacy of Mayan culture. Although aspects of the calendrical system, and the numbering system on which it is based, predate the Maya of the Classic Period (250–900 CE), it was their genius and expertise with numbers and astronomy that brought the Mayan calendar to its peak of sophistication – a refinement that, in certain ways, is still well in advance of our own calendar more than a thousand years later.

A calendar enables a culture to place in its history important events such as births and deaths, times when rulers took or lost power and dates of battles. These events make up the history of a culture and also define the people's relationship with their gods, with the powers that govern their existence. For the Maya, time was a manifestation of the gods, along with every other aspect of creation, from the Earth to the celestial objects of the heavens. The recording of time was therefore a sacred process. Numbers had a religious identity, intimately related with the passage of time. The 'time technology' of the Maya came to pose difficult questions for those who study their achievements. How did they develop such a sophisticated system? What does it tell us about their advanced understanding of the world, the solar system the universe? And are there aspects of Mayan time prophecy that we need to comprehend in our modern world?

# Numbers

*Our understanding of the Mayan calendar and numbering system is based on the work of the 19th-century researchers. These professionals and amateurs decided to decode the few Mayan texts that had survived the ruthless purges of the Spanish invaders and their desire to erase all traces of cultures that they regarded as demonic.*

*All numbers in the Mayan system had their own sacred function related to time. In this codex page, the important number 13 appears multiple times.*

## Source material

Indeed, without the surprising and often lucky discoveries of early academics and enthusiasts such as Alfred Maudsley, Lord Kingsborough and Charles Etienne Brasseur de Bourbourg, perhaps everything we now know and value about the Mayan system of time and thought might have been lost. Even Bishop Diego de Landa, who later wrote an account of the Maya, was initially responsible for the destruction of many Mayan texts following the arrival of the conquistadores: 'We found a great many books and because they contained only superstitions and the lies of the devil we burned them, to which they reacted most terribly as it gave them much pain.'

Only four Mayan codices ultimately survived the Western purge – the Dresden, the Paris, the Madrid and the Grolier. All four codices are painted on bark paper that was whitened with lime. They are all folded, concertina-like. It is generally thought they were produced in the Post-Classic Mayan period, somewhere between 1200 and 1520, although they may have been copied or adapted from earlier manuscripts. These texts, and carvings on stone stelae, have become the source material that has gradually revealed the secrets of the Mayan calendar.

## The vigesimal counting system

In their use, expression and manipulation of numbers, the Maya were the most advanced civilization of their time. Apart from the Hindus, who used zero for astronomical calculation, the Maya were the only people to actively make use of the concept of zero in their mathematical and calendrical systems. For this, they employed the image of a shell, which was presumably intended to portray emptiness.

Where we now use a decimal counting system based on the number ten, the Maya used a system based on the number 20 – this is known as a vigesimal system. As we shall see, the use of the vigesimal counting system is a key feature of the calendar known as the Long Count, which lies at the heart of the Mayan understanding of time.

Seen in texts and carvings on stone, Mayan numbers are expressed in written form using the vigesimal numbering system, which utilizes dots to represent one or units of one, lines as five and a shell shape to express the concept of zero. So after four dots are reached, the line is employed to denote five and further dots are added to make six, seven, eight and nine, until two lines make up ten, and so on. Once 20 is reached, this is expressed using the shell symbol with a dot above it, in the same way that the figure 10 in the decimal system uses the 1 to denote a ten and the 0 to denote the number of units.

## The positional system

This concept in a mathematical counting regime is called a 'positional' system. In other words, it means that a small number of symbols can be given different values depending on their position. The decimal system that we use is a good example of a positional system: in the number we write as 55, we have the same symbol used in two different positions – one to indicate five (or five units), and the other to indicate 50 (or five tens). In the Long Count system of the Maya, numbers increased by 20-fold when they were moved from a 'lower' position to a 'higher' position.

In fact, there is an important anomaly in the Mayan system of day counting, which means that although 20 *kin*, or days, make up the basic month, or *uinal*, it is then 18 (rather than 20) *uinal* that make up the *tun*, or basic 'accounting' year of 360 days. Beyond this, the system returns to its vigesimal order, with 20 *tun* making up the *katun* of 7,200 days, or almost 20 solar years, and 20 *katun* making up the *baktun* of 144,000 days, or roughly 394 years and four months. It is 13 of these *baktun* periods that make up the full 5,125 Gregorian years and approximately 132 days of the Mayan Long Count calendar, the most recent of which started on the 13 August 3114 BCE and will end on 21 December 2012.

When Long Count dates appear on stone stelae, they appear in a number of very particular forms. One of the earliest Long Count dates, from the Epi-Olmec period, on Stela C at Tres Zapotes shows a simple version of the Long Count: counting from an introductory glyph at the top, the numbers appear in their simple bar-and-dot form. From the top they read: 7.16.6.16.18; this means 7 *baktun*, 16 *katun*, 6 *tun*, 16 *uinal* and 18 *kin*. This adds up to a total of 1,125,698 days. Counting from the start date of 13 August 3114 BCE, this dates the stela's Long Count to 1 September 33 BCE.

Before we look at the Long Count calendar in greater depth, we need to understand the other building blocks of the Mayan calendar: the 260-day Tzolkin and the 365-day Haab'.

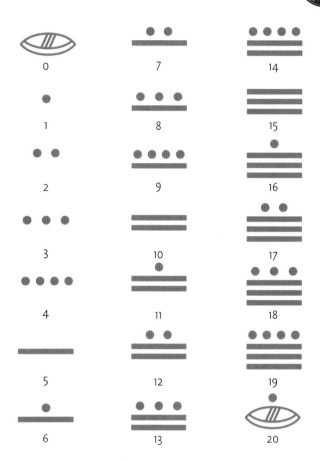

**The Mayan numerals**
The Mayan numbering system is vigesimal – based on the number 20, as opposed to our decimal system which uses ten as a base.

# The 260-day Tzolkin calendar

*At the very heart of the Mayan calendrical system is the 260-day period known as the Tzolkin, or sacred calendar. The Tzolkin certainly predates the Classic Maya period and some experts believe it was established by the Olmecs as early as 3000 BCE, although the first inscriptions – from the Zapotec region of Monte Alban near Oaxaca – would appear to date from between 700 and 500 BCE.*

### The numbers 13 and 20

The 260-day period is the product of two numbers – 13 and 20 – both sacred to Meso-American culture. As we have seen, 20 is important because it represents the 'number base' of the Mayan counting system. Where the modern world now has a decimal system based on the number ten, the Maya and their forefathers based their counting on 20 – it has been suggested that they chose 20 because it is the number of fingers and toes on the human body, although the absolute origins are no clearer than this (interestingly, the Maya were the only culture to have developed such a system).

*The Dresden Codex records accurate astronomical information about the solar and lunar eclipses, the Venus cycle and the Mars cycle – all recorded using the Mayan 'bar and dot' numbering system.*

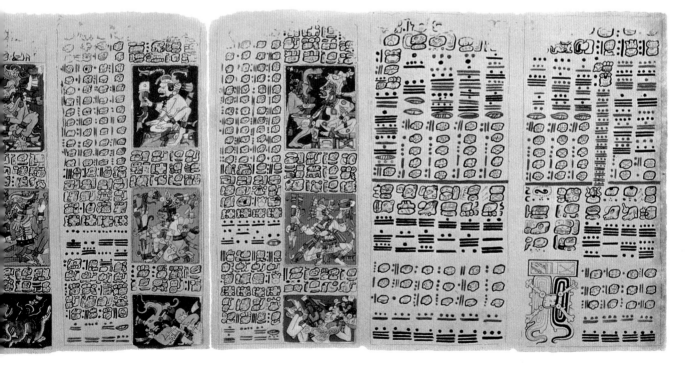

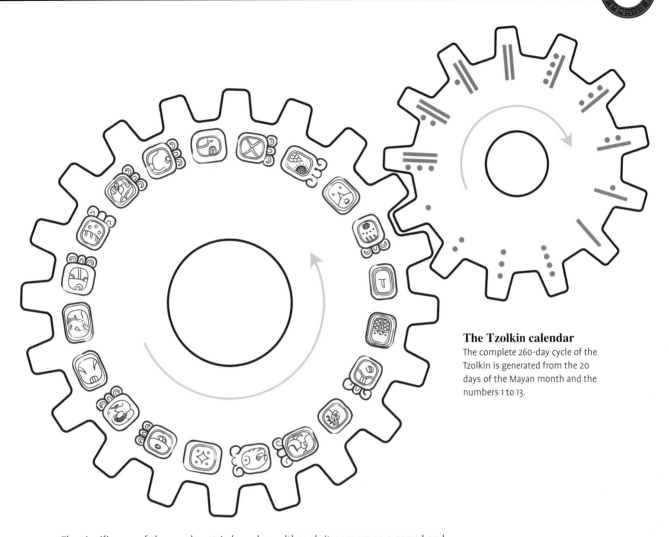

**The Tzolkin calendar**
The complete 260-day cycle of the Tzolkin is generated from the 20 days of the Mayan month and the numbers 1 to 13.

The significance of the number 13 is less clear, although it appears as a sacred and important number throughout the world. It is used extensively throughout the Mayan calendar, but despite various competing theories about its source, the overriding importance of 260 as the key sacred number may justify the choice of 13 as the 'implicit' multiple of 20. As some people have observed, the choice of 260, or '13 times 20', may be a question of which came first: chicken or egg, number or significance?

Each of the 20 elements in the Tzolkin calendar was given both a name and a graphic symbol, now known as a 'glyph'. Glyphs of different kinds appear throughout the Mayan calendar, including glyphs for days and months and glyphs with other specific meanings.

## The 20 day glyphs
The 20 day glyphs that appear in the Mayan codices are named in sequence: Imix, Ik, Ak'bal, K'an, Chikchan, Kimi, Manik', Lamat, Muluk', Ol, Chuwan, Eb, Ben, Ix, Men, Kib, Kaban, Etz'nab, Kawak and Ahau.

Each glyph has a specific meaning or meanings, which were (and still are) significant to the Maya people and form part of the Mayan language system (see box below). These descriptions are not definitive and understanding of the glyphs is open to interpretation. In one sense they are small mandalas (symbols of the universe), which the Maya considered to be alive and which embodied energies that, once encountered, could take on a powerful and instructive life within a person.

## Tzolkin predictive qualities

Within the Tzolkin, the glyphs and the numbers combine in an interesting way that appears at first counter-intuitive. In our own system we start the year on 1 January, and the following day we change only one of these elements – the number of the day – to 2 January. However, in the Mayan system the first day, 1 Imix, is followed by 2 Ik, which is followed by 3 Ak'bal, 4 K'an, and so on, with both elements increasing by one until the numbers complete (and restart) their cycle of 13 and the glyphs also complete (and restart) their cycle of 20 at 8 Imix. This progressive flow of glyph and number can be best understood as two interlocking wheels (see page 73), one with 13 numbers and the other with 20 day glyphs. As these rotate, they produce 260 different possible combinations of number and day, until one Tzolkin is completed at 13 Ahau; the next day, the 260-day cycle begins again with 1 Imix.

In this way each day within the 260-day Tzolkin calendar has a specific identity, and a person's birthday would be given a special significance and interpretation in Mayan culture. It is also known that the 260-day Tzolkin was strongly linked to prediction. Each of the 260 days was considered auspicious for certain activities and not for others. There are still Maya Daykeepers in Guatemala who provide predictive services to individuals, based on an understanding of the Tzolkin calendar and the relationship between the person's birthday and other events that may be occurring at certain times – in much the same way that a Western or Chinese astrologer will provide similar information. This aspect of prophecy, prediction and augury is – and always was – at the heart of the Mayan calendar.

## Meanings of the day glyphs

- Imix – crocodile, caiman or dragon
- Ik – wind or air
- Ak'bal – night or house
- K'an – lizard, corn or seed
- Chikchan – serpent
- Kimi – death or world-bridger
- Manik' – deer or hand
- Lamat – rabbit or star
- Muluk' – water, rain or moon
- Ol – dog
- Chuwan – monkey
- Eb – grass, tooth or human
- Ben – corn or reed
- Ix – jaguar
- Men – eagle or wise one
- Kib – vulture, owl or warrior
- Kaban – earthquake or the Earth itself
- Etz'nab – knife or mirror
- Kawak – storm or rain
- Ahau – lord, the ancestors and the sun

IMIX  IK  AK'BAL  K'AN  CHIKCHAN

KIMI  MANIK'  LAMAT  MULUK'  OL

CHUWAN  EB  BEN  IX  MEN

KIB  KABAN  ETZ'NAB  KAWAK  AHAU

## The Tzolkin day glyphs

The 20 day glyphs are still important in
the contemporary Mayan world and many
people identify with the glyph of their
birthday in the same way that we may
look to the zodiac month of our birth.

# Why 260 days?

*The first and most obvious question concerning the Tzolkin calendar is: why 260 days? By exploring why the full Tzolkin cycle includes 260 days, we can discover more about the Maya and their understanding of the world and the wider universe.*

In his book *The Maya*, M.D. Coe questions the origins of the Tzolkin: 'How such a period of time ever came into being remains an enigma, but the use to which it was put is clear. Every single day had its own omens and association, and the inexorable march of the twenty days acted as a kind of fortune-telling machine guiding the destinies of the Maya and all the peoples of Mexico.'

### 260-day cycles

But there are those who have questioned the origins of the enigmatic Tzolkin and want an answer that will satisfy them. It might be an interesting starting assumption that the 260-day Tzolkin was linked to natural cycles that the Maya saw occurring in the world around them. But what were these cycles? Certainly the life cycle of maize, from planting to harvest, can be very close to 260 days and it is well established that maize was the staple diet of the Maya.

An even more interesting and convincing idea is that the period of human gestation, from the mother's first 'missed' menstrual period to birth, is on average close to 260 days. Given also that the Tzolkin was considered to be so closely connected to a person's birth and their personality, the link – or identity – between conception and birth (particularly for those who are astrologically inclined) is a tempting one.

### Astronomical connections

What about the links to the astronomical cycles that we know fascinated the Maya? To the modern eye, the number 260 may, at first sight, appear to be astronomically arbitrary. It is certainly a long way from the solar year of 365.242 days and clearly the Tzolkin is of a wholly different nature. As we shall see, the Maya also used the Haab' calendar (a 365-day 'vague year') and an 'accounting year', a 360-day period called the *tun*. However, the Tzolkin calendar held – and continues to hold – a huge and quite different significance for the Maya.

Knowing the Maya and their overwhelming interest in astronomy, it is worth investigating the potential significance of the number as it occurs in celestial cycles. Venus shows itself as both the evening and morning star, and some researchers have attempted to link its cycle to the 260-day period. In his 1980 book *Skywatchers of Ancient Mexico*, Anthony Aveni says that the morning- and evening-star phases of Venus in the skies last, on average, 263 days. However, John Major Jenkins, the author of a book entitled *Cosmogenesis 2012*, states that the Dresden Codex sets the length of the Venus cycle (between its first rising in the morning and its first rising in the evening) at 258 days. Archeo-astronomer and academic Vincent H. Malstrom put forward the

*Page 34 of the Madrid Codex associates the timing of events with astronomical observations. A priest is shown planting maize at an annual ceremony, while at the top of the page, on a black background, is the famous Skywatcher of the Yucatán.*

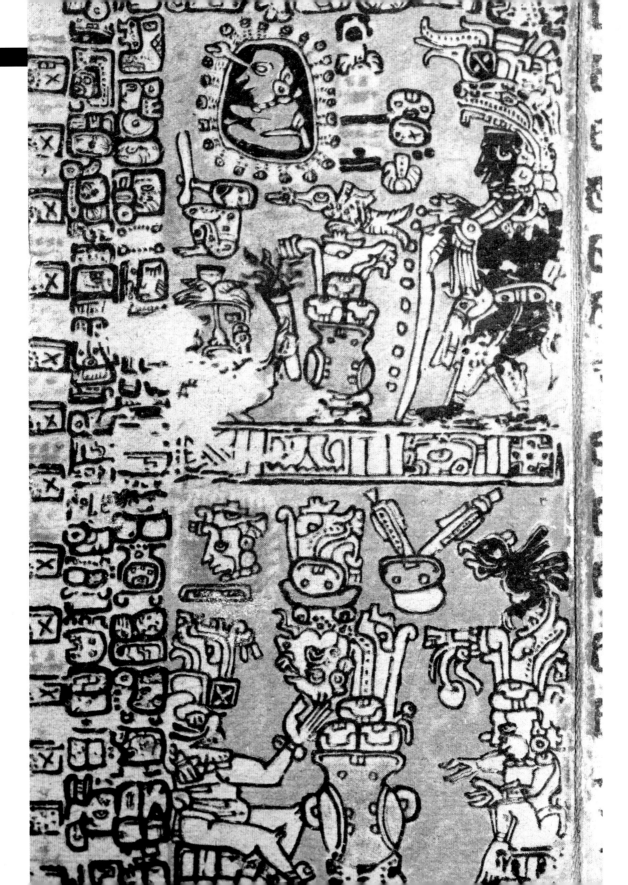

## Segment of the 260-day cycle

The 260-day Tzolkin, each day a combination of a number and one of the 20 day glyphs, formed the Mayan 'sacred calendar'. Even today divination is carried out by Maya Daykeepers using the Tzolkin calendar.

7 AHAU

6 KAWAK

5 ETZ'NAB

4 KABAN

3 KIB

2 MEN

1 IX

13 BEN

12 EB

11 CHUWAN

10 OL

9 MULUK'

8 LAMAT

7 MANIK'

6 KIMI

5 CHICKCHAN

4 K'AN

3 AK'BAL

2 IK

1 IMIX

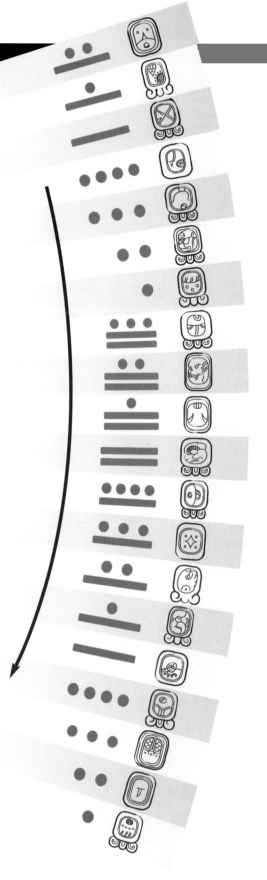

theory in 1973 that there was a 260-day interval between the zenithal sun at the Mayan observatory at Copán, some 15 degrees north of the equator. It is also true that three eclipse half-years are equal to 519.93 days, which is remarkably close to two Tzolkins.

These are all interesting pieces of evidence on their own, but they don't necessarily bring together all of the Maya's interests in one sacred number. What we do know is that the Maya had an abiding interest in a total of five celestial cycles: the solar cycle or 'tropical year', the Venus year cycle, the lunar month, the Mars year and the Jupiter year.

## Whole-number cycles

In his paper 'The Mayan Calendar – Why 260 Days?', author and researcher Robert D. Peden puts forward a cogent argument to show how the 260-day cycle is the only possible whole-number cycle that can accurately synchronize these five other cycles observed by the Maya, in order to give an accuracy of better than one day in 100 years (see box). Any system has to be based on whole numbers because the Maya do not appear to have had a grasp of fractions or parts of numbers.

As well as showing that only the period of 260 days can bring together these multiples of other astronomical cycles so accurately, Peden demonstrates that the Mayan Long Count calendar (see page 84) is a lunar calendar with an accuracy of 0.8 days (about one hour and 55 minutes) in 100 years.

Taken together, these facts argue strongly that the sacred Tzolkin calendar has a basis in astronomical observation and mathematical calculation, and demonstrate once again the sophistication and extraordinary achievements of the Maya.

## Synchronizing the calendars

Peden put forward the following equivalences to prove that the 260-day Tzolkin cycle is the only whole-number cycle to accurately synchronize all other Mayan time cycles:

- 59 sacred 260-day cycles (15,340 days) are equal to 42 'tropical' solar years, with an error of just four hours in the 42-year period, or about 9½ hours over 100 years; also important is the fact that 59 is a significant Mayan number, being the whole-number length of two lunar months

- 405 lunar-month cycles (each of 29.5306 days) is equal to 46 Tzolkin periods, or 11,960 days, with an error of just over seven hours in 100 years

- 61 Venus years (on average 583.922 days) is equal to 137 Tzolkins, or 35,620 days, to within 20 hours over 100 years

- One Mars year (on average 779.936 days) is equal to three Tzolkins (780 days), with an error of 2.8 days over 100 years

- 88 Jupiter years (each of 398.867 days) is equal to 135 Tzolkins, to within about seven hours over 100 years.

# The solar calendar: the Haab'

*The Mayan Haab', or 'vague year', was 365 days long and was clearly a conventional solar calendar that matched the observations of the spring and autumn equinoxes to within a day. The vague year was composed of 19 months: 18 of these were 20-day 'months', followed by a five-day period of uncertainty or unlucky 'intercalary' days, called the Uayeb.*

## Meanings of the 18 month glyphs

Various meanings have been given for these glyphs. The set of general meanings provided by Mayanist Christopher Jones in 1984 is as follows:

- Pop – mat
- Uo – black conjunction
- Zip – red conjunction
- Zotz' – bat
- Tzec – unknown
- Xul – dog
- Yaxkin – new sun
- Mol – water
- Chen – black storm
- Yax – green storm
- Zac – white storm
- Ceh – red storm
- Mac – enclosed
- Kankin – yellow sun
- Muan – owl
- Pax – planting time
- Kayab – turtle
- Kumku – granary

The use of the 20-day period echoes the Tzolkin's 20-day period and is another example of the Mayan vigesimal system (see page 70). It seems clear that the 18 months, each lasting 20 days, in the Haab' calendar (a 360-day period also known in the Long Count as the *tun*) were simply the closest 20-day multiple to the solar year.

## The 18 month glyphs

As with the Tzolkin, the Haab's 20-day months are all given both a name and a glyph, as is the five-day Uayeb. The 20-day months were counted from zero to 19 and were named Pop, Uo, Zip, Zotz', Tzec, Xul, Yaxkin, Mol, Chen, Yax, Zac, Ceh, Mac, Kankin, Muan, Pax, Kayab and Kumku.

The Uayeb – the five unlucky days at the end of the 365-day Haab' – was believed to be a time when the barriers between the mortal world and the underworld broke down and it became impossible to prevent evil deities from creating disasters. During this time many people would avoid leaving their homes and refrain from washing and combing their hair, for fear that bad events might befall them.

## The Haab' as a 'wandering year'

The counting of the vague year was not like the Tzolkin: the days of each month were numbered sequentially and, rather than starting on the first of the month, actually began on the zero, also known as the 'seating' of the month. In this way the days would run: Seating of Pop, 1 Pop, 2 Pop, 3 Pop... all the way through to 4 Uayeb, the final day of the 365-day year.

At 365 days in length, the Haab' is really identical to the ancient Egyptian 'wandering year'. Within a few years the inaccuracy of the missing quarter-day would put the Maya out of step with the seasons. However, many experts believe that, with their sophistication, the Maya would have had a mechanism for correcting this aberration. For as we have seen from the origins of the Tzolkin, the notion of the vague year should not imply that they were approximate in their counting or that they did not have an accurate length for the solar year. Calendars that record time passing – by the

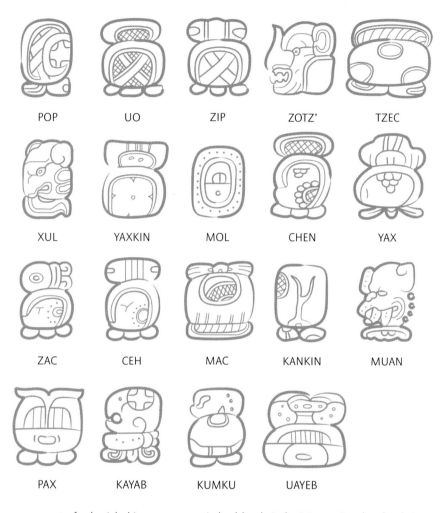

|  |  |  |  |  |
|---|---|---|---|---|
| POP | UO | ZIP | ZOTZ' | TZEC |
| XUL | YAXKIN | MOL | CHEN | YAX |
| ZAC | CEH | MAC | KANKIN | MUAN |
| PAX | KAYAB | KUMKU | UAYEB | |

**The Haab' calender**

The Haab' glyphs remained similar throughout the Maya Classic era. Some representations of the glyphs appear to include both astronomical and seasonal information, and may contain colours that relate to the four directions.

movement of celestial objects – are not judged by their 'basic' counting, but by their ability to make systematic adjustments to bring the calendar back into synchronization with the cycle they are tracking.

The concept of the leap year is a good example: every four years we readjust our Gregorian calendar to resynchronize with the Earth's orbit around the sun. This would be fine if the cycle of the Earth's travel around the sun were exactly 365.25 days. But this is not close enough to the actual cycle of 365.2422, so we therefore have to adjust by a further day every 100 years (unless the year number can be divided by 400 to give a whole number) by *not* having the leap-day creation of 29 February. In other words, 2000 (divisible by 400) *was* a normal leap year, while 2100, 2200, 2300 will not be leap years. This is still not perfect and actually gives a figure of 365.2425 (a plus error of .0003), so that further adjustments are made at longer intervals – further apart than 400 years – to bring us back into synchronization with reality. As we shall see, this error in our contemporary Gregorian calendar is actually greater than the error accepted in the Mayan calendar.

# Measurement of time cycles

*'Intercalary' adjustments – the insertion or deletion of extra days in the calendar to make it more accurate – are key to understanding the Mayan calendar, for in searching for a number that was significant in relation to their lives, the Maya were not simply staring at the sun. As we have seen, they had an interest in a total of five celestial cycles: the solar year, the Venus year, the Mars year, the lunar month and the Jupiter year.*

*Discovered buried beneath the temple at Palenque, this mask of the sun god was once set into an outer wall, where it was venerated.*

From their choice of 260 days for the Tzolkin, many Mayan scholars now believe that their measurement for the tropical solar year was actually more precise than our current Gregorian approximation of 365.2425, which demands that a leap day is added for 97 out of every 400 years. In actuality, the real length of the tropical solar year – the time it takes for the Earth to return to the same point in its solar orbit – is 365.2422.

## Mayan intercalation

Some researchers have put forward the idea that the Maya used their own form of intercalation based on their own important numbers to provide an answer that was more accurate. This was founded on the idea that an average tropical year is 365 days plus 63/260ths of a day – or 365.2423 days. This intercalation requires a total of 25 days to be added every two Calendar Rounds (104 years), plus one extra day every ten Calendar Rounds (520 years). If this were applied, it would mean that the Mayan calendar contained effectively only one-third of the error inherent in the Gregorian leap-day system – a system that post-dated it by many years.

In terms of the correspondence between the Tzolkin and the solar tropical year, it is also interesting to note that 59 Tzolkins is very close to being exactly 42 solar years. In fact, there is an error of just four hours and 19 minutes.

When the 260-day cycle of the Tzolkin is synchronized with the 365-day vague year, we initiate a further cycle that only first completes itself 52 years later. By specifying a date within the Tzolkin cycle and the vague year – say, 3 Ben 7 Pop – it is possible to locate a specific day within the 52-year period. So 3 Ben 7 Pop occurs only once within the whole 52-Haab' Calendar Round and fixes the exact day on which a particular event occurred.

## The Calendar Round

The combination of the 260-day Tzolkin calendar and the 365-day Haab' calendar gives rise to a longer cycle, lasting 52 Haab' years, called the Calendar Round.

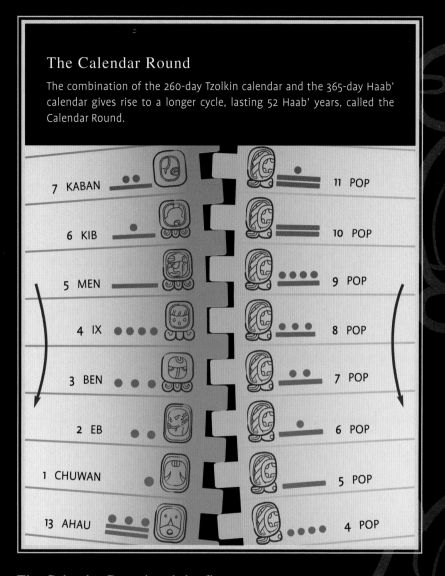

| 7 KABAN | 11 POP |
| 6 KIB | 10 POP |
| 5 MEN | 9 POP |
| 4 IX | 8 POP |
| 3 BEN | 7 POP |
| 2 EB | 6 POP |
| 1 CHUWAN | 5 POP |
| 13 AHAU | 4 POP |

## The Calendar Round and the fire ceremony

The 52-Haab' Calendar Round was an important cycle for the Maya and for the Aztecs, who adopted the same basic calendar as the Olmecs. After this period they would have known from observations that their solar calendar was 12 days out of synchronization, and it was at this point – an event that most Meso-Americans would probably have seen only once in their lifetimes – that they performed a fire ceremony to ward off the possibility that the sun would not rise again. This ceremony lasted 12 days and was an intercalary period to put their calendar back in sync with the true solar calendar. As we have seen, using this intercalation was actually part of process by which the Maya could make their calendar more accurate than our current Gregorian calendar.

# The Long Count calendar

*Although considered by many the great achievement of the Maya, the Long Count calendar is likely to actually predate their civilization. It enabled them to place an event on any day within a period of 1,872,000 days, or nearly 5,125 solar years – the duration of one of their ages. This current age (which began in 3114 BCE) is, according to the Maya, the fifth age of creation and follows four other ages of creation and destruction of the same duration.*

### Future ages?

This begs the question whether the Maya believed there are further ages to come, such as the sixth, seventh, eighth and so on. There is some evidence to suggest that each age of 5,125 years is actually part of a larger cycle, similar to the idea that each of the Western astrological ages – such as Aquarius, with a duration of 2,150 years – is one-twelfth of the larger precessional cycle known as the Great Sidereal Year, which lasts for around 25,800 years. John Major Jenkins, in his book *Maya Cosmogenesis 2012*, maintains that the Maya considered the fifth age to be the final age, the Age of the Jaguar.

This idea is disputed, however, by the evidence that is found on a monument in Coba, some 96 km (60 miles) from Chichén Itzá. Here we find a number that is 28,697,869,473,684,210,526,315,784,000 Mayan years (of 360 days each) – showing a clear expectation of a long, almost infinite future to come.

### Discovery of the Long Count

In 1867 a librarian from Danzig named Ernst Förstemann took up a job in the Dresden Library, where by chance the most important Mayan text was resident. The Dresden Codex (see page 43), some 75 pages of glyphic language, had for hundreds of years eluded decoding, and by 1880 the codex had become Förstemann's obsession. He made 60 facsimiles of the original wood-bark text – an act that, in retrospect, had a profound effect on our understanding of the Mayan calendar, since the original was seriously damaged by water while being stored in a wine cellar during the Second World War bombing of the city.

Working with the Dresden Codex and a copy of Bishop Diego de Landa's *Rélacion de las Cosas de Yucatán*, Förstemann discovered the main workings of the Mayan calendar. He revealed the vigesimal (base-20) number system (see page 70) and the fundamental workings of the Long Count calendar based around the number 20. He also discovered the workings of the Mayan 52-year Calendar Round and the date of the Long Count's start at 4 Ahau 8 Kumku, thousands of years ago.

### Dating objects using the Long Count

The first unequivocally Mayan artefact is often thought to be Stela 29 at Tikal, which records a Long Count date of 8.12.14.8.15, locating it in 292 CE.

*The Dresden Codex was the key document in the decoding process of the Mayan Long Count calendar and opened the door to their cosmology. This page shows a section of a* tonalmatl *– another name for the sacred period of 260 days that was at the centre of the Mayan calendar system.*

## How the Long Count works

From Förstemann's work we now know the many ways in which the Maya parcelled time and the name each of these parcels was given:

• A day was called a *kin*

• 20 *kin* made up a *uinal*, the Mayan month

• 18 *uinal* made up a *tun*, the 360-day 'year' (the only departure from the 20-base number system that occurs in the Long Count)

• 20 *tun* made up a *katun* of 7,200 days

• 20 *katun* made up a *baktun*, lasting 144,000 days, 400 Mayan years or just over 394 solar years.

There is scope within the Long Count for the number of *baktun* to reach 20, giving a period of 8,000 Mayan years, but in practice the Great Cycle of the Mayan Long Count calendar is only 13 *baktun* long – 1,872,000 days, 5,200 Mayan *tun* years of 360 days, or 5,125 solar years and 133.725 days.

Often in Mayan stelae, the carving is topped with a large introductory glyph to tell us to expect a Long Count date. Below this are two columns of glyphs. Working from left to right and top to bottom, the first five of these glyphs provide the Long Count date, while further glyphs also give the date according to the 260-day sacred Tzolkin and the 365-day Haab'.

Each of the five glyphs of the Long Count incorporate the number, set vertically on its left side as well as the glyph image of the god, to indicate the *baktun*, *katun*, *tun*, *uinal* and *kin* (see box). These glyphs developed in style, complexity and meaning across the Mayan kingdoms, and different versions and subtle variations can be found at the major city sites.

The image from the Leyden Plate – a jade plaque discovered in 1864 by workmen digging a canal close to the Guatemalan coast – shows a typical Long Count date. It reads from top to bottom, starting with the introductory glyph, which tells us that what follows is a Long Count date. The next five glyphs, together with their numbers on the left of the glyph, reveal their Long Count elements: 8 *baktun*, 14 *katun*, 3 *tun*, 1 *uinal*, 12 *kin*. This is followed by two further number/glyph combinations, which give its Tzolkin identifier as 1 Eb and its vague-year identifier as 0 (or Seating of) Yaxkin, the seventh month. In modern terminology, the three parts of the Long Count are shown as 8:14:3:1:12 1 Eb 0 Yaxkin.

Glyphs as a varied form of writing and recording history developed during the flourishing of the Mayan culture, and such is the complexity of the imagery that it has taken many years of painstaking work to begin to unravel them. At first researchers believed they were merely 'pictograms' that expressed ideas graphically, but eventually it was realized that the glyphs are a form of written speech, which includes symbols for syllabic sounds as well as visual concepts.

*Stone stelae, such as this monument at Tikal, were often used to record important events in the history of a city-state, together with their Long Count dates.*

# Why 13 *baktun* in a Great Cycle?

*For the Maya, 13* baktun *was the length of a Great Cycle. Apart from the great myth, the Popol Vuh, they appear to have left little information about the previous Great Cycles. There are many who say that there have already been four Great Cycles in the current 26,000-year-long Great Year, each lasting 5,200 Mayan years or 5,125 solar years.*

### The Four Suns of the Vaticano-Latin Codex

The Aztecs, who lived parallel to the Maya and also outlived the Classic Maya period, had their own idea of the Great Cycles. Both peoples believed there had already been four ages and that we are now in the Fifth Great Cycle or Fifth Sun.

In the Aztec document known as the Vaticano-Latin Codex, the previous four suns are described: the First Sun, Matalactli Atl, was overseen by the goddess of water Chalchiuhtlicue, She with the Jade Skirt. The age lasted 4,008 years, and those who lived in this time ate water maize called *atzitzintli*. In this age lived the giants, but this First Sun was destroyed by water in the sign Matlactli Atl (10 Water). It was named Apachiohualiztli (deluge, flood, the art of sorcery of the permanent rain). It is said that humans were turned into fish, and some say that only one couple – named Nene and Tata – managed to escape, and protected themselves in an old tree living near the water. Another version states that there were seven couples who hid in a cave until the flood was over and the waters had gone down. They repopulated the Earth and were worshipped as gods in their nations.

The Second Sun was called Ehecoatl and lasted 4,010 years. The people who lived then ate wild fruit called *acotzintli*. This sun was destroyed by the wind serpent known as Ehecoatl and humans were turned into monkeys. Only one man and one woman, who stood on a rock, were saved from destruction in the year Ce Itzcuintli (1 Dog).

*Chalchiutlicue was consort of Tlaloc. She oversaw 'horizontal water' such as lakes, rivers and seas, and was responsible for the age of the First Sun.*

*Patecotl the pulque god and Ocelotl the jaguar warrior are portrayed in the 15th-century Aztec Vaticano-Latin Codex.*

The Third Sun was called Tleyquiyahuillo and lasted 4,081 years. This age was populated by the children of the man and woman who had survived the destruction of the Second Sun. They ate a fruit called *tzincoacoc*. This age was destroyed by fire.

The Fourth Sun, Tzontilic, lasted 5,026 years and at the end of this period humans died from starvation after a deluge of blood and fire.

The Vaticano-Latin Codex acknowledges us to be within the Fifth Sun today, and it was the possibility of the coming end of the Fifth Sun that drove the Aztecs to violent and insane levels of human sacrifice – killing 80,000 people in one ritual alone and more than 250,000 in one year by the beginning of the 16th century.

# The Aztec Sun Stone

*The Aztec Sun Stone, or 'calendar stone' as it is sometimes inaccurately described, is possibly the most important surviving Aztec artefact. This 24.5-tonne (24-ton) piece of carved basalt is understood to have been carved in 1479, under the auspices of the Aztec priesthood, but was not 'rediscovered' by the Spanish until 1790, during the renovation of el Zócalo, Mexico City's central plaza.*

Its intricately carved, coded information has gradually been revealed through the work of Aztec scholars and now tells us much about the Aztec picture of time and how closely it matches the Mayan calendar. The focus of the stone is the central face of Tonatiuh, the sun god. His tongue, it is thought, is actually a sacrificial flint or obsidian knife, and on either side of his head are two claws, each holding a human heart from a sacrificial victim. Around the god's face are four quadrants, each representing one of the previous four ages and the god that oversaw its destruction. Interestingly, as is demonstrated in the box below, the story as told by the Sun Stone does not exactly match the version in the Vaticano-Latin Codex (see page 88).

## The four suns of the Aztec Sun Stone

According to most interpretations of the Sun Stone, the First Sun is represented by Ocelotonatiuh, the jaguar god. In the time of this First Sun there lived the giants who had been created by the gods, but who were eventually attacked and devoured by jaguars. The Second Sun is overseen by Ehecoatl, the god of air and wind. During this age the entire human race was destroyed by hurricanes and men were transformed into monkeys. The Third Sun is depicted as a deity with a head of rain and heavenly fires. In this era all creation was destroyed by a fire from the skies and flowing lava; every home was submerged in the fires and humans transformed themselves into birds to escape the cataclysm. The Fourth Sun was overseen by the water goddess Chalchiuhtlicue, and destruction came in the form of terrible rains and floods. Even the mountains were submerged and humans were transformed into fish.

---

### Comparison of the ages of the suns

Details of the ages of the four suns as inscribed on the Sun Stone vary from those recorded in the Vaticano-Latin Codex.

|  | Vaticano-Latin Codex | Sun Stone |
|---|---|---|
| First Sun | Apachiohualiztli; age ended by deluge and flood, humans turned into fish | Ocelotonatiuh; age ended by jaguars |
| Second Sun | Ehecoatl; age ended by winds, humans turned into monkeys | Ehecoatl; age ended by winds, humans turned into monkeys |
| Third Sun | Tleyquiyahuillo; age ended by fire | Deity with head of rain and heavenly fires; age ended by lava and fire, humans turned into birds |
| Fourth Sun | Tzontilic; age ended by starvation after deluge of blood and fire | Chalchiuhtlicue; age ended by deluge and floods, humans turned into fish |

## The Fifth Sun

But what of our own time, the Fifth Sun? Tonatiuh is the central, circular sun god who awaits sacrifice and desires the blood and the hearts of humans. He and all the other images of the ages are pictured within the motif known as Ollin, which signifies movement. Does this mean that these are all stages of evolution and movement, or is there a more specific meaning indicating that all these changes are associated with movement of the Earth, perhaps even with changes of the Earth's rotation on its axis or in its magnetic make-up?

The Aztecs believed that Tonatiuh, the Fifth Sun, was already very old – hence his wrinkled face – and some gave a start date as far back as the fourth millennium BCE, without providing a duration or an end-date. All they knew was that their role was to try and postpone the end of the Fifth Sun by continuing to feed Tonatiuh with his seemingly insatiable diet of human sacrifice.

Although scholars have attempted to decode accurate calendrical information from the artefact, the Aztec Sun Stone does not appear to date the ages of the five suns. Mayan scholar Karl Taube has claimed that the central image contains the date Nahui Ollin – the creation of the Fifth Sun, which the Aztecs believed occurred at the ancient city of Teotihuacán, just 40 km (25 miles) north-east of Mexico City. For whatever reason, only the Maya could put a date on the end of the fifth age: 21 December 2012.

It is also interesting to compare the Aztec Sun Stone with the lid of Pacal the Great's tomb at Palenque. Some scholars, such as Maurice Cotterell, claim that the lid shows a different description of the five ages, in which the Fifth Sun represents the age of the jaguar, rather than the age of the sun god Tonatiuh.

*The Aztec Sun Stone – which is yet to be fully decoded – contains a history of the world in five suns. This huge artefact is now the key exhibit in Mexico City's Anthropological Museum.*

# Correlation and accuracy of the calendar

*At least initially, the barrier to efforts to correlate the dates of the Long Count with European calendars based on the Gregorian system was the lack of data from Mayan monuments showing dates linked to other known events. Often these artefacts were hidden deep in the jungle out of the sight of serious researchers. Alfred Maudsley, the first major surveyor of Mayan inscriptions, provided the information, but did not solve the correlation problem.*

## Deciphering of the calendar

In 1897 an eccentric American journalist and entrepreneur named Joseph T. Goodman published his first findings about the Mayan calendar. While he did not mention Förstemann's name, few people believe that Goodman was unaware of the German's great achievements. But for Goodman's readers, it would appear that he had deciphered the entire calendar and had proposed the beginning of the Long Count at 4 Ahau 8 Kumku.

In 1905 the journal *American Anthropologist* published a paper entitled simply 'Maya Dates', in which Goodman's ideas about the correlation of the Mayan and Gregorian calendar first appeared. From his study of Bishop de Landa's *Rélacion de las Cosas de Yucatán*, the codices and other colonial records, Goodman came to a figure that was, in fact, incorrect by two days. Nevertheless it would take some years before Goodman's closeness to the truth was confirmed, first by Juan Martinez in 1926 and then in 1950 by the prominent Mayanist Eric Thompson. This 'GMT-2' correlation established the start of the Long Count (0.0.0.0.0) on 11 August 3114 BCE and the end-date (13.0.0.0.0) on 21 December 2012. (The date of 3113 BCE is often seen: this is an error introduced because there is no year called 0. The European 'historical' Gregorian calendar goes directly from 1 BCE to 1 CE. In fact the two forms are often distinguished by using the correct suffix: so, for example, 3113 BCE 'astronomical' is the same as 3114 BCE 'historical'.)

So we can say that, in the Mayan system, 12.19.17.19.19 is the day before 13.0.0.0.0 4 Ahau 3 Kankin, the beginning of the sixth age in Mayan mythology, which is due to begin (depending on the exact correlation) on 22 December 2012, exactly 1,872,000 days, or 5,200 *tun*, after the fifth Great Cycle began.

## The accuracy of the calendar

The Tzolkin's length at 260 days provides some extremely accurate conclusions, when integrated with observations about various celestial cycles such as the solar tropical year, the lunar month and the Venus year. It is still not clear, however, which came first: the 260-day Tzolkin or the observations?

Many scholars now believe that the desire for accuracy in their observation of the cycles was not the main aim of the Maya. Rather it was their wish to find out how the sacred Tzolkin fitted with all the cycles that they witnessed around them.

It was Ernst Förstemann who first discovered that the Dresden Codex contained detailed astronomical tables that provided Mayan priests with information to enable them to predict the solar and lunar eclipses. These tables contained observations that were carried out over long periods of time: in the case of the eclipse table, 11,960 days. In fact it is not necessary to record for this length of time simply to establish the intervals between eclipses, but the Maya had other reasons for their dedication. The purpose of this length of observation was to discover when the Tzolkin cycles interlocked with the cycles they were recording. For instance, 11,960 is exactly 46 Tzolkin, as well as being exactly 405 lunar months. In fact, calculations show that the Mayan value for the lunar month was only seven minutes too short, and that a further calculation contained within the codex provided a correction that would enable the lunar calendar to remain accurate to within one day every 4,500 years.

Förstemann also discovered that five pages of the Dresden Codex were given over to tables of observations of Venus. As part of its data, the Venus table in the Dresden Codex also records the cycle of 'heliacal' rise – the point when the sun and Venus rise together – as a raw average figure of 584 days, whereas the true figure for the average Venus year is 583.922 days. But, as we have seen above, 61 of these accurately averaged Venus years is equivalent to 137 Tzolkin, with an error of only some 16 hours over nearly 100 solar years.

It is thought that the Dresden Codex's religiously accurate observations were made at the numerous observatories that the Maya erected throughout their lands, the most important being the remarkable Caracol at Chichén Itzá (see page 104). Looking through the pages of the Venus table, one cannot but imagine the dedication of the priest-observers as they tracked the sacred spheres day upon day, year upon year.

*Stela D from the Classic Maya site of Quirigua in Guatemala contains the Long Count date of 9.16.15.0.0. or 566 CE. Over 4.5 metres (15 feet) high, the stela demonstrates some of the finest glyph carving in the Mayan world.*

# Chapter 5

# ASTRONOMY, DESTINY AND PROPHECY

When the Maya looked up at the skies they saw the gods. The sun, the moon, the stars and the planets were living deities that had influence over every aspect of their lives. By their movements, these deities measured out time in the universe. Time, therefore, belonged to the gods, just as all life belonged to the gods. The Maya knew they owed their lives to the actions of the gods and were willing to honour and reverence them at every opportunity, for they feared the gods as the agency of their misfortunes.

Every celestial event was the cause of corresponding terrestrial events. Every person was under the influence not only of their birthday in the 260-day Tzolkin, but of other celestial cycles. Each day was auspicious for certain activities and inauspicious for others, and these interpretations were the preserve of the Mayan priests and Daykeepers. As astronomers, they studied the long-term cycles of the heavens too, looking for the clues that would tell them about their fate, not just as individuals, but as members of a tribe, part of the human race and aspects of the whole Earth's creation. But how accurate were their prophecies? Were they really accurate enough to predict events many hundreds of years into the future of humankind?

# Prophecy

*Prophecy was always at the heart of Mayan culture, and the ability to know the future was highly prized among the Mayan elite. Those whose profession it was to understand and predict coming events were known as* chilan, *which means that they were interpreters of the gods. Because of their knowledge they were held in high esteem and this was reflected, quite literally, in the fact that they were carried on the shoulders of men when they travelled about their lands.*

*Eat, eat, thou hast bread;*
*Drink, drink, thou has water;*
*On that day, dust possesses the Earth,*
*On that day, a blight is on the face of*
   *the Earth,*
*On that day, a cloud rises,*
*On that day, a mountain rises,*
*On that day, a strong man seizes the land,*
*On that day, things fall to ruin,*
*On that day, the tender leaf is destroyed,*
*On that day, the dying eyes are closed,*
*On that day, three signs are on the tree,*
*On that day, three generations hang there,*
*On that day, the battle flag is raised,*
*And they are scattered afar in the forests.*

From the Book of Chilam Balam of Tizimin

*Divination rituals appear in many art forms including polychromatic vases such as this example from Tikal in Guatemala.*

## Talking with the gods

Their methods were obscure, esoteric and mysterious. In the Book of Chilam Balam known as the Tizimin manuscript, however, the process that a *chilan* used to communicate with the gods is described. He would first go to a particular room in his house, where he would lie prostrate and induce a trance state. Once he was in this altered condition, the god or spirit would come to the house and rest on its ridge pole, from where he would speak to the *chilan*, who would speak or channel the information he received from the divine source; the other *chilan*, who assembled in the next room, would listen and record the message with their heads bowed.

## Types of prophecy

Generally Mayan prophecies fall into four types: day-prophecies for individual days within the 260-day Tzolkin; year-prophecies based on the 365-day Haab'; *katun*-prophecies based on the 20-year period; and, finally, special prophecies about the return of Kukulkán, the Plumed Serpent avatar – or Quetzalcoatl as the Aztecs called him.

## Day-prophecies

These were mostly confined to the Maya *ah-kinyah*, or diviner, who offered divination for the 260 different days in the Tzolkin, giving advice as to whether certain days were auspicious or not for particular kinds of activities or undertakings – for example, whether 1 Imix was lucky or unlucky for the sowing of certain crops or for embarking on a trading mission. Information about this kind of divination existed within all the Books of Chilam Balam, except the Book of Chumayel.

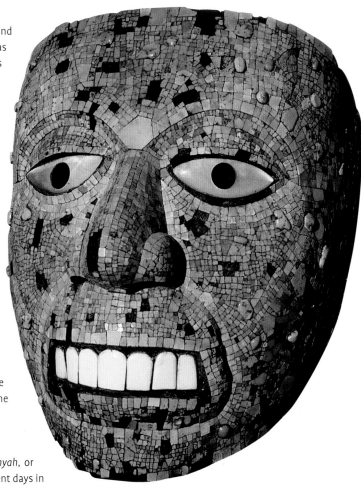

*A certain amount of prophecy was focused on the intervention in Mayan life of the god Quetzalcoatl, here represented in a highly refined mosaic mask.*

## Year-prophecies

Predictions for the particular Haab' years would certainly have been the work of the *chilan*. In the Books of Chilam Balam known as the Book of Tizimin and the Book of Mani there are two sets of parallel prophecies for the 20-year period of a *katun* named 5 Ahau. Although it is not completely clear to which Gregorian years these refer, each year is influenced by a particular deity and, in general, is a catalogue of misfortunes that are to be visited on the people. Famine, drought and plagues are foretold, as are wars, inter-city conflicts, the taking of prisoners and deaths in many forms. The books also detail the religious ceremonies that must be undertaken to ameliorate the effects of these forecast events.

# *Katun*-prophecies

*A katun lasts 7,200 days or just under 20 years, and many of the prophecies contained in the Books of Chilam Balam are* katun*-prophecies. They are not as pessimistic as the year-prophecies and are quite different in character. They were written using a Latin script, but it has generally been well attested that they represent a true translation from the original Mayan hieroglyphics.*

### Father Avendaño and the prophecies

The authenticity of the *katun*-prophecies is confirmed in a report by the missionary Father Avendaño, who worked closely with the Maya during the later part of the 17th century:

> *I told them that I wished to discuss with them the old means they use to reckon the days, months, years and ages, and to discover what age the present one might be (because for them an 'age' consists of just twenty years) and what prophecy there was about the present year and age; all this is recorded in certain books a quarter of a yard high (9 inches) and about five fingers broad, made of tree bark, folded from side to side like screens and each leaf as thick as a Mexican Real of eight coin. These are painted with assorted figures and characters on both sides, which show not only the count of the days, months and years, but also the ages and prophecies announced to them by their idols and images, or, to speak more accurately, the devil by means of the worship which they pay to him in the form of some stones.*

### Bishop de Landa's account

Another account by Bishop de Landa in 1556 expands on the theme of *katun* and the significance of the prophecies:

> *Not only did the people have a count for years and months... but they also had a particular method of counting time and their affairs by eras, which they counted in 20-year periods, counting thirteen times twenty... They name these periods* katuns. *In this way it was easy for the Elder to recall past events which had taken place as long as three hundred years before. As to who it was that put together this count of* katuns: *if it was the*

*evil one himself, it was done so as to serve his honour; if it was created by a man, he must have been a great idolator, for into these* katuns *he added all the deceptions, auguries and prophecies by which these people lived and breathed. This was the 'science' that they held to most firmly, the one which they held in the highest esteem.*

## The 'record of the *katun*'

In the Books of Chilam Balam there are two series of *katun*-prophecies, each covering a 13-*katun* period, which make up the *u kahlay katunob* or 'record of the *katun*'. In each 'record of the *katun*', the *katun* period is identified by the date of its final day, as it is known in the Tzolkin. This means that a 13-period *katun* record starts with *katun* 11 Ahau, which is the first *katun* in the series because it begins on the day 1 Imix – the first day of the sacred Tzolkin. The *katun* record now follows a defined cycle: 9 Ahau, 7 Ahau, 5 Ahau, 3 Ahau, 1 Ahau, 12 Ahau, 10 Ahau, 8 Ahau, 6 Ahau, 4 Ahau, 2 Ahau and ends with *katun* 13 Ahau. This period of 13 *katun* (93,600 days or roughly 256 years) is the smallest period into which both the *katun* of 7,200 days and the sacred Tzolkin of 260 days are divisible. The 'record of the *katun*' is also sometimes referred to as the Short Count, to distinguish it from the Long Count calendar of 5,125 years, which ends in 2012.

It is important to understand that the Books of Chilam Balam represent both an historical record and a prophecy of things to come, for the Maya believed that the world moved in cycles and that what had gone before would come again.

*A carved stela from Santa Lucia Cotzumalguapa in Guatemala is typical of the Early Classic period. All rulers and priests were expected to have a superior sense of what the future held for their people.*

*Codices such as the Madrid Codex were an attempt to establish causal links between celestial events and their effects on earth.*

## The 11 Ahau prophecy

The Book of the Chumayel describes the first prophecy for *katun* 11 Ahau:

> Katun *11 Ahau is established at Ichcaanzihoo [Merida]. Yax-haal Chac is its face [the Green Rain God, lord of the* katun*]. The heavenly fan, the heavenly bouquet shall descend. The drum and rattle of Ah Bolo-yocte [the regent or priest of the* katun*] shall resound. At that time there shall be the green turkey; at that time there shall be 'Zulim Chan'; at that time there shall be 'Chakanputun' [symbols of times when the people were driven from their homes into the forest]. They shall find their food among the trees; they shall find their food among the rocks, those who have lost their crops in* katun *11 Ahau.*

## Thompson's summary

Interpreting the Books of the Chumayel and Tizimin, Sir Eric J. Thompson made a translated summary of the prophetic characters of the first series of *katun* described in the Books of Chilam Balam:

11 Ahau – niggard in the *katun*; scanty are its rains... misery
9 Ahau – drought, famine
7 Ahau – carnal sin, roguish rulers
5 Ahau – harsh his face, harsh his tidings
3 Ahau – rains of little profit, locusts, fighting
1 Ahau – the evil *katun*
12 Ahau – the *katun* is good
10 Ahau – drought is the charge of the *katun*
8 Ahau – there is an end of greed; there is an end to causing
  vexation... much fighting
6 Ahau – shameless is his speech
4 Ahau– the Quetzal shall come... Kukulkán shall come
2 Ahau – for half the *katun* there will be bread; for half the *katun* there
  will be water

*This clay figurine from Palenque portrays a person of high caste. His meditational pose, together with his headdress, suggest that he is involved in prophecy.*

## The coming of the conquistadores

Research by Mayanist Ralph L. Roys now indicates that this first series of Chumayel *katun*-prophecies refers to the 13th century, and that the *katun* 4 Ahau is dated to the period between 1224 and 1244. The second series of prophecies relates to a later time, and elements appear to foretell the arrival of Christianity and the Spanish conquistadores. Bishop Diego de Landa states in his *Rélacion de las Cosas de Yucatán* of 1556:

> *As the Mexicans had signs and prophecies of the Spaniards' coming...*
> *so did the people of the Yucatán. Some years before being conquered by*
> *Admiral Montejo, in the district of Mani, in the province of Tutul Xiu,*
> *an Indian named Ah cambal, who held the office of* chilan...
> *announced that they would soon move to new calendar bearers and*
> *would be ruled by a foreign race who would preach a God and*
> *the virtue of wood which he called* Ua hom che. *This meant*
> *'a tree raised up, of great power against the demons'.*

The implication of the bishop is clear: the Maya had been waiting for the arrival of Christian Spaniards bearing the True Cross of Jesus.

## Special prophecies

Chilam Balam was an inhabitant of Mani and lived during the reign of the ruler Mochan Xiu. It was in *katun* 2 Ahau – around 1500 – that Chilam Balam made an incredible prediction: he said that in the next 20-year cycle known as *katun* 13 Ahau, bearded men would come from the east and bring a new religion to the Maya people. The Book of the Chumayel records the prophecy in detail:

> *The prophecy of Chilam Balam, Mani, the singer of Cabal-chen. On the day of 13 Ahau, the* katun *will end in the time of the Itzá [a tribal people of the Yucatán, in the time of Tancah (Mayapan)], Lord. The sign of Hunab-ku [the one god] is on high. The raised wooden standard will come. It will be displayed to the world, so that the world may be enlightened, Lord. There had been a beginning of strife, there has been a beginning of rivalry, when the priestly man will come to bring the sign in the time to come, Lord.*
>
> *Receive your guests, the bearded men, the men from the east, those who bear the sign of God, Lord. Truly good is the word of God that comes to us. The day of our regeneration is coming…*
>
> *The First Tree of the World [the world tree, a symbol of the cosmos associated with the Christian cross by the Maya] is restored; it is displayed to the world. This is the sign of Hunab-ku on high. Worship it, Itzá. Today you will worship his sign on high. Furthermore, you will worship it with true goodwill… You will be converted to the word of Hunab-ku, Lord; it came from heaven.*
>
> *Believe in my word itself, I am Chilam Balam and I have interpreted the entire message of the true God.*

## Manipulation or prediction?

There has been some controversy as to whether the prophecies in the Books of Chilam Balam were manipulated by Spanish missionaries who were involved in translating or transliterating the texts and were keen to show that the prophecies foretold the arrival of Christianity. Why the missionaries would want to use the apparent supernatural powers of Satan-worshippers to validate their claim to spiritual supremacy is, in itself, debatable. Nevertheless there are those who believe that the prophecies were 'shifted' in time to make predictions about the arrival of the Spanish fit in with history.

For those who trust the source, it seems clear that Chilam Balam himself believed he was foreseeing the return of Kukulkán/Quetzalcoatl and his group of white-robed priests and that these events were imminent. The *katun* 13 Ahau was due to start in around 1520 and end in our year of 1539. The best estimates of Chilam Balam's personal history locate his main prophecies around 1500, just 19 years before Hernan Cortés' arrival in Mexico.

There is an even more extraordinary prophecy about *katun* 13 Ahau to be found in the Books of Chilam Balam, which was apparently written down during the 11th century by the *chilan* known as Ah Xupan Nauat. Not only does the *chilan* predict the arrival of white men in the lands of the Maya, but he also states that this event will take place during the eighth year of *katun* 13 Ahau, or 1527. This is astonishingly accurate dating, for it was in the year of 1527 that Francisco de Montejo – who was later to be titled Capitan-General of Yucatán by King Carlos 1 of Spain – arrived for the first time on the east coast of the Yucatán peninsula.

*A page from the 1579 manuscript* History of the Indies *by Diego Duran shows Spanish Caravels arriving at the coast of the Yucatán.*

# Sky-watchers of the Yucatán

*The Maya needed to understand the astronomical cycles so that they could honour the gods by holding rituals at the most appropriate times. They were setting up appointments with the gods that they wished to keep: their greatest fear was that if they did not observe these passings in the correct ways, significantly bad events would befall them. So how was it possible for the Maya to become such advanced astronomers? What instruments did they use?*

Some Mayan scholars have identified what they believe to be 'architectural instruments' that would have been used as observatories, where the Maya could have made recordings of celestial cycles over long periods of time. As we have seen, the Maya were interested in a series of astronomical cycles: the solar year, the lunar month, the Venus cycle, the Mars cycle and the Jupiter cycle. It would have been possible for them to measure the solar cycle, its equinoxes and solstices using sight-lines on buildings and the well-known 'E-groups' of building configurations, such as the one at Uaxactun (see page 35).

## The Caracol at Chichén Itzá

For the more complex cycles of the moon, Venus and Mars, many experts believe the Maya used other kinds of buildings that have been dubbed 'observatories', even though the exact ways in which they were used is still a subject of enquiry. One of the most impressive and fascinating of all Mayan buildings is the Caracol at Chichén Itzá. Even in its partially ruined state, the building looks very much like a modern observatory that would hold a giant telescope. Its name actually means 'snail' in Spanish and refers to the narrow winding staircase that leads to the damaged upper tower, which sits on the larger, now-eroded 'dome' that was once cylindrical in shape.

The whole Caracol structure sits on an upper platform and a larger, lower platform, some 52 by 67 metres (170 by 220 feet) which, together, raise the entire structure above the flat but dense Yucatán foliage. From the top of the Caracol, the Maya would have had unobstructed views of the heavens and of quite distant horizons. The platform on which it stands is not exactly square, but is laid out in a way that gives rise to a number of highly significant alignments.

The first of these is a diagonal alignment, which – in a manner similar to Stonehenge in Wiltshire, England – means that the corners of the platform, as viewed from the centre of the observatory tower, line up with the summer-solstice sunrise in the north-east and the winter-solstice sunset in the south-west.

The next significant aspect of the building is the orientation of the main entrance staircase, built at an angle of 27.5 degrees north of west. This angle is not part of any other alignments at the Chichén Itzá site and seems to have been reserved for this building. The most obvious reason is that this angle has an important relationship with the planet

Venus, for it represents the most northerly extreme of Venus' position in its unusual cycle, and is a point visited only once by the planet every eight years.

Another aspect of the staircase is that it appears to have been built to receive what is called the 'zenith passage' sunset. The zenith of the sun occurs when the sun is directly overhead – something that only happens inside the central band of the Earth known as the Tropics. For locations within this area, the zenith occurs twice within one year – the time gap between the two events depending on the latitude of the location. At Chichén Itzá, which is at a latitude of about 20 degrees north, the two zenith passages take place around 26 May and 20 July. On these two days the sun passes directly overhead Chichén Itzá and nothing vertical casts a shadow. Everything is ruled by the sun, and at these times it is both literally and metaphorically at its most powerful.

*Built around 1000, the Caracol's tower has specially aligned windows that provide siting lines for a large number of different celestial events.*

*One of the most unusually shaped buildings in the Mayan world, the Observatory at Monte Alban is unique in having no two sides or angles the same. Its orientation appears to have been related to important stellar events.*

## El Castillo, Chichén Itzá

The most dominant building at Chichén Itzá is El Castillo, the great pyramid dedicated to the sun god, the Plumed Serpent Kukulkán. Built into the structure of the building is an extraordinary trick that demonstrates much about the Maya, their culture and their understanding. At sunset on the equinoxes on 21 March and 21 September the sun hits the balustrade wall on the north stairway and casts a shadow that ripples down the entire pyramid, terminating in the huge serpent head at the base of the wall. In this extraordinary interaction between light and matter, a grand, almost magical illusion renews the life of Kukulkán, the Plumed Serpent of the Mayan world, the solar lord.

## Monte Alban, Oaxaca

Although not strictly a Mayan site, Monte Alban, which lies close to Oaxaca, contains many of the same Zapotec influences that formed later Mayan culture. Generally believed to have been built between 100 BCE and 200 CE, the Observatory at Monte Alban is also known to archeologists as Building J. It stands out from the remainder of the buildings there for a number of reasons: first, it is oriented at about 45 degrees east of north, quite different from most of the other structures; more important, however, is the building's strange asymmetry. Unlike the symmetrical configuration of many Meso-American ritual buildings, the Observatory seems to have no two walls with the same measurements and no angles that are common to all sides.

Stone plaques along the back walls of the building appear to show figures with sighting sticks and other astronomical references. They seem to have been collected together from a number of different locations, further indicating that this building was created for a special purpose. A number of significant star alignments are claimed for the building by archeo-astronomers who have studied the position of the stars at the time when the building was created. Another building on the site, Building P, contains a stairwell with a sight-tube similar to the Zenith Tube at Xochicalco (see below).

## The Governor's Palace, Uxmal

At Uxmal, some 113 km (70 miles) west of Chichén Itzá, the building known as the Governor's Palace carries a hieroglyphic 'throne inscription' above its central doorway, which has attracted great interest among Mayanists and archeo-astronomers. Part of the doorway carries depictions of zodiac constellations.

## The Zenith Tube, Xochicalco

At Xochicalco, in the small Mexican state of Morelos, the Mayan inhabitants built an artificial cave observatory with a special feature to record the zenith passages of the sun. A tubular solar chimney, some 4 metres (13 feet) high, links the cave to the world above. The stone-lined tube, which is only about 30 cm (12 inches) across, is absolutely vertical. This means that only when the sun is directly overhead – at noon during the two zenith passages each year – can the sunlight reach down the tube to the floor of the cave. Not only would this have given the Maya information about the solar year, but it would have provided important cues in the planting cycle of their staple crop, maize.

*On the stairs of Building P at Monte Alban there is access to a room that is illuminated by the sun twice a year at the times of the solar zenith. In the valley of Oaxaca this occurs on 2 May and 10 August.*

# Astronomical achievements

*As we know, just four glyph books survived the purges of the Spanish invaders: the Dresden, the Paris, the Madrid and the more recently discovered Grolier Codex, which is still, to some Mayanists, a disputed text. Often referred to as 'priests' manuals', the three undisputed codices contain all the information required by the priests to make auguries and prophecies.*

*Rattlesnakes twist up and down across a number of pages in the Madrid Codex. Some experts believe these pages are an attempt to link astronomical events to rainy seasons.*

It has become clearer to modern epigraphers working on their decipherment that, as well as encoding information about rituals and almanacs relating the importance of the 260 days in the Tzolkin, the codices' most important achievements were in the recording of astronomical information – something that is not recorded in any other surviving Mayan artefact. We will never know how much more was known and recorded in the many books that Diego de Landa watched being burned on his destructive bonfires.

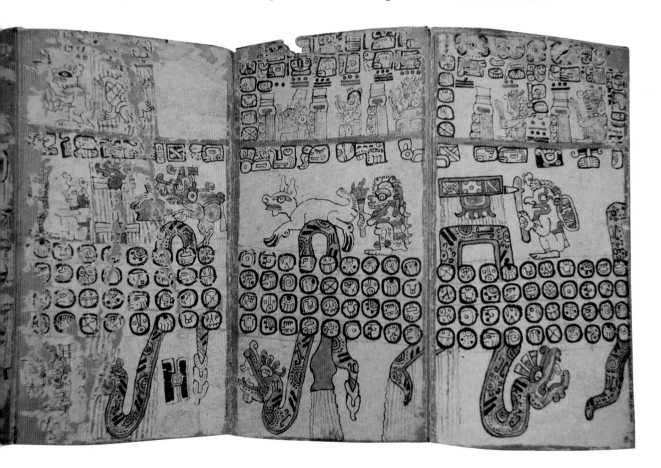

## The Dresden Codex tables

The most complete, and perhaps the most thoroughly understood, of the surviving codices is the Dresden Codex, which, from its glyphic style, is believed to have originated from an area close to Chichén Itzá or Tulum in the Yucatán. It also contains a Long Count date that correlates to 755, but may well have been a document that was copied from generation to generation, and the information contained within it may have been recorded many years earlier. Despite recent advances in decoding and understanding inscriptions at various Mayan sites, the Dresden Codex still represents the best guide to the astronomical achievements of the Maya.

In brief, it contains three remarkable tables, which each occupy many pages. The first is an eclipse table that predicts when lunar and solar eclipses will occur – itself an incredible feat of observation and calculation. The second is a Venus table, which predicts when Venus will rise as the morning star, the time known to us as the heliacal rise of Venus. Then there are two separate Mars tables – one that records the times when Mars goes into retrograde motion, and another (only recently decoded) that follows Mars' movement along the ecliptic.

## The Dresden eclipse table

Although Ernst Förstemann had studied the Dresden Codex and had uncovered the existence of the Venus table in 1901, the eclipse-predicting nature of the lunar table was only identified by Martin Meinshausen in 1913. It took until 1924 for American scholar Robert Willson to fully understand its workings. The lunar table – as well as the Venus and Mars tables – perfectly expresses the Mayan obsession with prophecy and the synchronization of celestial events and their sacred 260-day Tzolkin calendar. It tracks the movements of the moon through 405 lunar months, or 11,959 days, according to the table. This is one day short of 46 complete Tzolkin cycles, which is 11,960 days, and implies that the Maya understood this synchronization. With modern techniques we know that 405 lunar months is exactly 11,959.89 days, which means that the Mayan value implies an inaccuracy of just 22 seconds for each lunar month – a stunning achievement without the use of telescopes or other technological equipment. It would have required accurate observations to be recorded for 32 years and nine months of our modern calendar: quite literally a religious observance.

Interestingly, an inscription on the Temple of the Sun at Palenque, and dedicated in 692, seems to equate 81 lunar months to 2,392 days – giving an average lunar month of 29.5308 days – just as in the codex.

The Book of Chilam Balam of Chumayel gives a dramatic, anthropomorphic description of a solar eclipse:

*The Sun is bitten into. What bites into it is that it is matched with the Moon, which goes attracted to it (the Sun), before biting it. It arrives through its path to the north, large, and when they become one and the Sun and the Moon bite each other, before arriving at the 'trunk of the Sun'. It is explained this way so that Maya men can understand what happens to the Sun and to the Moon.*

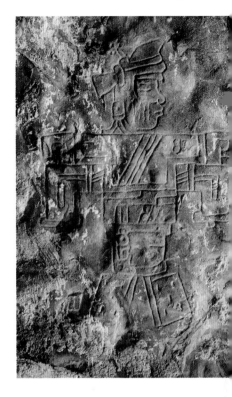

*Carvings from the outer walls of the Observatory at Monte Alban record victories over other cities and are also believed to represent astronomical symbols.*

## Foretelling 'dangerous' times

The main point of the eclipse table, however, was to be able to identify 'dangerous' eclipse times, at which appropriate rituals could be carried out to maintain cosmic order and ward off the risk of bad events brought forth by the gods. To demonstrate the accuracy of the eclipse tables, Mayanists Harvey and Victoria Bricker have been able to show that all 77 solar eclipses predicted in the 33-year cycle occurred within two days of their predicted dates. Of the 69 lunar eclipses predicted by the table, 51 of them took place within one day of their predicted 'dangerous' times.

## The Dresden Mars table

The Mayanist Robert Willson proposed in 1924 that pages 43–45 of the Dresden Codex contain a table that tracks the movements of the planet Mars. The pages include a variety of information: across the central portion runs a Tzolkin almanac that lasts for 780 days – very close to the 'synodic' period of Mars, the cycle that measures the closeness of Mars and the Earth. Curiously there are also four images of an animal that has become known as the 'Mars Beast' – a creature that also appears in the Madrid Codex. Suspended from a 'sky band', the cloven-footed animal has been variously identified by modern scholars as a hog or a deer; it is not readily identifiable with Mars, but no one deity has ever been exclusively associated with the Red Planet. Nevertheless, the creature's identity as the Mars Beast has stuck.

For some time, many scholars did not believe that the Mars table contained any astronomical significance, but in the 1970s and 1980s attempts were made to match the ten 78-day periods with the 75-day cycle in which Mars appears to travel backwards in space – its retrograde motion – though not all scholars are convinced that the Maya would have allowed such inaccuracy. Indeed, some experts have proposed that the numbers in the table may refer to the cycles of other planets, such as Jupiter or Saturn.

It is not yet known exactly what the text of the Mars almanac refers to, although it is possible that its predictions are a warning of dire happenings when Mars enters its period of retrograde motion, where the glyphs appear to indicate that 'The Mars beast was axed, damaged, sacrificed.'

*Right: The Temple of the Sun at Palenque is oriented towards the rising sun at the winter solstice. Inscriptions found inside have helped prove the astonishing accuracy of the astronomical calculations of the Maya.*

# Venus in the Dresden Codex

*It is hard to overemphasize the importance of Venus in the world of the Maya, and the pages referring to the planet in the Dresden Codex only serve to reinforce this. Venus appeared to the Maya as an unusually bright star – visible even during the day – but the early Meso-Americans must have been mystified by its apparently strange behaviour, which revealed its identity as an object that moved independently of the 'fixed stars' of the heavens. For the Maya, Venus became one of the most important objects in the skies and its influence over their actions was profound.*

### Venus as morning star and evening star

To understand why it was so significant, it is essential to first describe Venus' unusual motions from the perspective of an earthly observer. In its unique cycle, Venus starts its identity as the morning star: at daybreak it rises, at first just for a very short time, but then gradually each day it rises for a little longer, goes a bit higher in the sky and shines a little brighter, before its light is obscured by the rising sun. After 131 days or so it reaches its peak and starts to fall again, until after a further 131 days it fails to rise. Its role as the morning star is over after 263 days and it disappears from view. Its obscurity lasts for some 50 days before it is miraculously reborn as the evening star – a fact that made early observers believe that Venus was, in fact, two different celestial objects.

In the night sky, Venus begins to rise a bit more and shine a little more brightly each night for 131 days, until it starts to fall again for another 131 days or so, before again disappearing below the horizon. But this time its absence lasts just eight days, before it rises again as the morning star and restarts its lifecycle. In total this has taken close to 584 days – a duration known as the synodic period of Venus, or the Venus cycle. The Dresden Codex does not concur with the individual parts of the Venus cycle, but it does concur with the overall figure of 584 days. This was most likely due to Mayan difficulty in viewing its precise risings, but it did not affect their overall understanding of the Venus cycle.

### The Venus cycle and the solar year

It turns out that the Venus cycle has an interesting and intimate relationship with the length of the solar year, the time it takes the Earth to orbit the sun: 365 days. The ratio between 365 and 584 is almost exactly the same as the ratio 5:8. In other words, five Venus cycles equates almost exactly to eight years. Mayan sky-watchers would also have observed that Venus has a further eight-year cycle, which sees extremes in the northerly rising of Venus in the summer and in the southerly rising of Venus in the winter.

These are the kinds of facts that would have astonished the Maya, as the same time as they confirmed their sense of order in the cosmos. The Maya would have been fascinated to see what happened when these observations were tracked further out in time. Would the order remain in place? And how would the sacred Tzolkin of 260 days coincide with the cycles of the Earth and Venus? When we examine the Venus pages in the Dresden Codex, we can see the Maya pursuing these very questions and finding answers that confirmed their sense of a numerically ordered universe – the work of their gods. ○

## The Venus table

The Venus table is remarkable first of all for its sheer size: it starts on a rise of Venus on the Tzolkin date of 1 (hun) Ahau and continues through 65 synodic periods of Venus – that is, through 37,960 days, or exactly 104 Haab'-years and 146 Tzolkins, a period which for the Maya is an excellent synchronization of many cycles. It would clearly

*A detail of the Codex Cospi, an Aztec divinatory calendar, showing the planet Venus, known by the Aztecs as Tiauixcalpantecuhtli, attacking warriors. The figures on the left are year symbols.*

have taken the work of many generations to achieve such long-term observations, a duration that was crucial to reaching accurate conclusions about the average Venus cycle, which could vary between 581 and 587 days. As well as coming to an average whole-number date of 584 days, this long-term information also gave the Maya the methodology for making ongoing corrections, in order to bring their tables back into synchronization with the true behaviour of Venus.

On the limed bark of the folded codex, the Venus tables occupy six densely packed pages. Each page is divided in two: on the left-hand side is a table giving the dates of the risings and settings of Venus as the morning star and the evening star. On the right-hand side are the gods and the auguries associated with each of the heliacal rises of Venus, the key time when Venus first rises as the morning star with the sun.

The first Venus page gives the Long Count date where the user enters the table, as well as providing information for making corrections to the table when it is used at different times in the future. This makes it a foolproof, future-proof system for the priests who would have responsibility for observing the rituals and making the required prophecies that their rulers would demand. Perhaps more than at any other time, the Maya would sacrifice their victims at the moment just following Venus' daytime peak on the other side of the sun. But they also feared its heliacal rising.

# Venus: planet of destiny

*The Maya referred to Venus by a number of names. One of these was Chak ek or the Great Star, although as we have seen, the planet was also identified with Hunahpú, the Hero Twin (see page 63).*

*The Venus god was important to the Maya and is sometimes associated with Quetzalcoatl, or Kukulkán. This representation was discovered at Copán in Honduras.*

A report written by Spanish missionaries from central Mexico, known as the Manuscript of Serna, tells us that the native peoples 'venerated and made more sacrifices' to Venus than to any another being, apart from the sun. It goes on: 'The reason why this particular star was held to be so important by the lords and the people, why they measured their days by this star and showed reverence and offered sacrifices to it, was because these mistaken natives believed that when one of their main gods, named Topilzin or Quetzalcoatl, died and left this world, he transformed himself into that resplendent star.'

## Venus and the sun

The Mayan equivalent of Quetzalcoatl – Kukulkán – appears in the Venus pages of the Dresden Codex. From early on in Mayan development, prior to the Classic period, Venus and its relationship with the sun were important symbols of authority and power. In the Mayan creation myth, the Popol Vuh, the Hero Twins Hunahpú and Xbalanque, who made the present world possible, were identified with Venus and the sun. And in the Venus pages of the Dresden Codex, the two headed Mayan monster has one head marked with Venus symbols and the other with solar symbols.

There is a simple logic for the link between Venus and the sun, for, even if the sun is much larger in the sky, the Maya would have known that the movements of both through the heavens had an important and close relationship. They would also have witnessed the transits of Venus when, for a few hours, just twice every 120 years or so, the small planet drifts across the face of the sun like a little boat crossing a lake.

This unusual astronomical activity seems to have made the Maya wary of the planet Venus and its cycle. It is known from post-conquistador manuscripts that on the heliacal rise of Venus, native people 'prepared a feast, warfare and sacrifices'. Another document expresses Mayan fears: 'And so, when Venus is in the skies, they know that he casts his light on certain people, those born on certain day signs, venting his anger against them, shooting them with darts.'

## The war star

As more and more inscriptions at Mayan sites have gradually been decoded, it has become clear that many wars among the city-states were timed to coincide with the rise of Venus. At Bonampak (see page 58) the extraordinary murals record an important victory on the Long Count date of 9.18.1.15.15 (16 August 792), within one or two days of the heliacal rise of Venus. The most recognizable glyph to express the idea of war also incorporates the glyph that means Venus. Even in the Dresden Codex, the Venus pages show Venus gods carrying spears with which to wound their victims.

*Immanuel Velikovsky believed that the Greek myth in which Athena (Venus in the Roman version) is born from the head of Zeus (Jupiter) recorded a real celestial event in which a piece of the planet Jupiter broke off to become Venus.*

## The 'birth of Venus'

As further decodings are made, it seems likely that they will both confirm and develop our understanding of the Venus influence over the Maya. In recent years the English Mayan researcher and author Maurice Cotterell has courted controversy with his theories about the significance of various aspects of the Mayan calendar. He maintains that the 'Maya Great Number' of 1,366,560 days that is found in the Venus table is vital to understanding the cycle of the planet and that of the sun.

For Cotterell, the number is significantly close to his own 'super number' of 1,366,040 (just 520 days, or exactly two *tun* different from the 'Maya Great Number') that measures a major cycle in solar activity. He believes that this variation in activity has caused great fluctuations in human fertility, which have seen the collapse of major cultures such as that of the Maya. Though not everyone agrees with his theory, he maintains that the solar cycle is strongly linked to the event known to the Maya as the 'birth of Venus', which marked the start of this age. Cotterell understands that the 'birth of Venus' was actually an event caused by the sun's extreme activity around 3113 BCE. This activity was so powerful, he maintains, that Venus tilted on its axis and started its 'reverse' orbiting direction.

## Velikovsky's theories

It is true that Venus is the only planet in the solar system that rotates the 'wrong way'. Also – and without necessarily agreeing with him – Cotterell cites the work of Russian writer and astronomer Immanuel Velikovsky. In his 1950 book *Worlds in Collision*, Velikovsky claimed that the planet Venus was literally 'born' from Jupiter – as a piece of matter spat out into the solar system following the impact of a comet on Jupiter's surface. His evidence for this is contained in a number of parts. His first point was that the large red spot on Jupiter was actually the scar where the matter that became Venus had somehow been gouged from the surface.

Velikovsky used myths and legends as part of his evidence. In the Greek myth of Athena, the goddess (who is identified with Venus in the Roman pantheon) springs from the head of Zeus (Jupiter), causing Mount Olympus to tremble and the seas to boil. Velikovsky believed that this myth told of a real astronomical event that was contemporaneous with the biblical Exodus of Moses and the Israelites from Egypt – something he thought happened in around 1500 BCE, rather than at the start of the Mayan Long Count calendar some 1,600 years earlier. He maintained that it was celestial events that caused the biblical plagues and the parting of the Red Sea, rather than any other more mundanely supernatural causes, such as the power of an Old Testament God.

Velikovsky also quoted Aztec and Mayan myths, including the central story of Kukulkán/Quetzalcoatl, the Plumed Serpent. He states that Quetzalcoatl was actually a well-used name among the Aztecs for Venus, or 'the star that smoked' as it was also called. And he draws on Bishop de Brasseur's *Histoire des Nations Civilisées du Mexique*, in which an ancient account of a major celestial event is recorded: 'The Sun refused to reveal itself and for four days the world was utterly deprived of light. Then a great star appeared: it was given the name Quetzal-cohuatl... To demonstrate its anger the sky caused many to die of famine and plague. It was at this time that the people calculated afresh the reckoning of days, nights and hours according to the difference in time created by the event.'

*The sponsor god of the Temple of the Cross at Palenque was known by a number of names: God GI, God K, Bolon Dzacab and Manikin Sceptre. While he was originally believed to be the sun god, many scholars now strongly associate him with the planet Venus.*

## Important questions raised by Venus

Could it really be – as some Mayan experts such as Cotterell believe – that this was the 'birth of Venus', the beginning of our current fifth age? If so, could such calamitous and galaxy-shaking events occur again?

When it was born, Velikovsky maintains, Venus was originally in a very different, more erratic orbit than it is now – travelling much closer to the sun, while still spinning as far out as Jupiter. This meant that it could pass relatively close to the Earth. During these close encounters, could Venus have caused the Earth to experience its own polar shifts and geomagnetic disturbances, which led to cataclysms on our planet? Cotterell uses various sources to argue for the existence of certain cataclysms in our past – catastrophes that fit with the reversing magnetic field of the sun, which he says occurs five times in 18,139 years. Could this really be the cause of a coming disaster in 2012?

# Chapter 6

# THE MESSAGE OF THE CALENDAR

When the Maya set up their Long Count, they knew that the conclusion of a great 13-*baktun* cycle was bringing many things together at one time. The culmination of a great age could always be expected to see life-changing, culture-transforming events. How could it not be so, when this is what had happened before? The gods were reliable in all things – especially their harvestings.

The Maya were naturally obsessed by cycles, by the interlocking nature of cycles and the increasing levels of importance that came with the synchronization of more and more cycles. That is why the end of the Long Count calendar on 21 December 2012 is an event of such epic proportions. But will this date be a time of destruction, confusion and negativity or a time of transformation that ushers in a new, more spiritual age? What is the message that the Maya left for us? And, apart from the calendar itself, what forms did their message take?

# The cult of the Plumed Serpent

*It is impossible to consider the message and meaning of the Mayan and Aztec cultures without talking about Kukulkán/Quetzalcoatl. The legends speak of Omeototl, the original 'dual' or couple god, creating Ehecatl in one breath. Ehecatl then gave birth to his own offspring, a son known simply as Son of Ehecatl. The father and son then merged into one being, one identity – a feathered or 'plumed' serpent.*

*At the spring and autumn equinoxes, the shadow cast on the Castillo at Chichén Itzá by the dying afternoon sun forms the rippling body of a snake that terminates in the stone Quetzalcoatl head.*

### A link to the divine

As a bird and a snake, Kukulkán links the Earth to the skies, the mundane to the divine. He is the great mystical mediator between realms, bringing the wisdom of the higher world to those of the lower world. Kukulkán ruled the western quadrant of the sky, while his brothers ruled the other quadrants: Yaotl the north, Xiuhtchutli the east and Huitzilopochtli, the solar god, the south. While some sources talk of him purely as a Mayan

deity – supernatural and completely above humanity, a metaphor like Zeus – there are others that give a more grounded picture of a wise man, a saviour, an enlightened one.

As a man-god, Kukulkán seems to have been as important to the history and development of Central America as Jesus Christ has been to the evolution of European culture. The two figures are in many ways very different, but there may also be interesting parallels that help us understand the role of the avatar or Master Teacher in the rise and fall of major cultures. They point to a perspective of 'Superior Wisdom' – of knowledge from a source not available to ordinary mortals. They also provide a sense of potential and possibility: 'What I have done, you shall do, and more,' Jesus Christ said. For the Plumed Serpent, feelings of humility, reverence and pride emanated from his followers. To be associated with this spiritual power was to be connected to the gods, to be linked to the eternal.

## Who, or what, was Kukulkán/ Quetzalcoatl?

Was the Plumed Serpent just a deity, or did he (like Jesus Christ, Buddha and Krishna) have a human or 'embodied' counterpart? Did he deign to give up his heavenly home and come to live among humans? And what role does he play in the message that the Maya left behind? Is it he who can tell us the meaning of the Mayan calendar?

The Books of Chilam Balam report that '...the first inhabitants of the Yucatán were the "People of the Serpent". They came from the East in boats across the water with their leader Itzamna, the "Serpent of the East", a healer who could cure by the laying on of hands, and who revived the dead.'

Bernardino de Sahagun, a 16th-century Franciscan friar and chronicler of the new land of Mexico, described Quetzalcoatl as more a man than a god: 'Quetzalcoatl was a great civilizing force who entered Mexico leading a band of strangers. He brought the arts to the country and was particularly important in encouraging agriculture. During his time the heads of maize were so large that one man might not carry more than one stalk at a time. Also, cotton grew in many different colours and so did not have to be dyed. He built spacious and elegant houses, and taught a religion that fostered peace among the people.'

Another early source tells a similar tale: 'Kukulkán arrived with nineteen companions, two of whom were gods of fish, two other gods of agriculture, and a god of thunder... They stayed ten years in Yucatán. Kukulkán made wise laws and then set sail and disappeared in the direction of the rising sun.'

*The god Quetzalcoatl is sometimes represented as a man with a serpentine divided tongue, as in this figurine from Teotihuacán.*

## Corroborative accounts

The Spanish chronicler Bartolomé de las Casas confirmed the story of the 20 men: 'The native people confirmed that in ancient times twenty men came to Mexico, their chief called Kukulkán... They wore flowing robes and on their feet were sandals. They had long beards and their heads were shaven... Kukulkán taught the people the ways of peace, and initiated the building of many important edifices.'

And the Spanish writer Juan de Torquemada told the same story in his *Monarchichia Indiana* of cultured people arriving with Quetzalcoatl: 'They were men of good bearing, well-dressed in long robes of black linen. These were open in front and without cape or cowl. They were cut low around the neck and had short sleeves that did not reach the elbow. These followers of Quetzalcoatl were men of great wisdom and knowledge and were skilled artists in many forms of fine crafts.'

## The end of a golden era

In many sources the idea is apparent that the arrival of Kukulkán – who is often portrayed as a white man – ushered in an age of peace and harmony, in which men and women lived happily in couples and there was an end to the human sacrifice that had been the signature of the earlier Olmec people. Instead, the new saviour encouraged animal sacrifice, provided laws, founded cities and organized communities. Importantly, Kukulkán also taught the ways of the calendar.

And yet, just as this seemingly golden age was flourishing, a shadow of evil descended on the land we now call Mexico. Some say there was a battle for the very soul of the Mexican people, during which Kukulkán's benevolence and humanity were pitted against the violence and brutality of Tezcatlipoca, a man-god (or, in some accounts, a deity pure and simple) who was also known as 'Smoking Mirror' after a magical object he would use to obtain secret knowledge. His ways demanded blood sacrifice of the human heart – an idea anathema to the Plumed Serpent. In some kind of cosmic battle, the two wizards fought for supremacy and Kukulkán was eventually beaten. His loss was not fatal, but he was expelled from the land of Tula, the ancient heart of the pre-Aztec, pre-Mayan peoples.

*Opposite: This image from the Mixtec codex known as Fejervary-Mayer shows Tezcatlipoca using his foot as a bait to tempt the Earth Monster to the surface of the great waters. The symbols in the lower part represent dates when Tezcatlipoca was dominant over other forces.*

*Below: Birds and other animals were often featured in Mayan art, not just as decorative motifs but as representations of important deities.*

## Arrival of the Spanish: return of Kukulkán?

In some accounts the defeated Kukulkán fled to the coast and sailed away in his ship without oars across the 'eastern sea', promising to return and restore justice and the rule of compassion. In the light of this, it seems less of a leap to understand the reaction of the indigenous peoples to the arrival of the Spanish, which for many represented the return of Kukulkán, as predicted. Just as Christians await the return of the Christ, so the Mexican native people awaited their saviour. Unfortunately for them, the Christians who came to their lands believed that if the natives weren't devils themselves, they were at least possessed by the Devil.

## Votan and Pacal

Some experts link Kukulkán to Votan, another mythical character believed to have arrived from across the sea. In his book *The Mayan Prophecies*, Maurice Cotterell puts the case for the identification of Kukulkán with Votan, a 'white man' who arrived across from across the eastern sea, or Atlantic Ocean. Bishop Nuñes de la Vega burned a book belonging to the Quiché Maya in 1691, but not before he had copied part containing a story about Votan, which was subsequently obtained by a friar named Ordoñez (see page 40).

The story told of a peaceful man named Votan, accompanied by attendants dressed in long robes. Votan was recorded making four journeys across the Atlantic to his original home, named Valum Chivim. Ordoñez believed that this city was Tripoli, now the capital of Libya, but then in Phoenicia. The legend also claimed that Votan made his way up the Usumacinta River and founded the great city of Palenque, perhaps as far back as 500–1000 BCE. This improbable and challenging story introduces the idea that the Americas were 'discovered' around 2,000 years or so before Columbus' first arrival. It also posits the theory that the culture of the Americas, and of the Maya in particular, was influenced by those familiar with the cultures of Egypt and Babylon. Could this explain the passion for pyramids on both sides of the Atlantic – a fact that has long fascinated archeologists?

Could it also be that Pacal the Great, the most remarkable of all the rulers of Palenque, was in some way connected to his forebear Votan? There are Mayan enthusiasts today, such as José Argüelles (see page 132), who refer to Pacal as 'Pacal Votan', as if his existence were predicated on his mythical forebear, who might also be connected to the lineage of Kukulkán.

These strange pieces of the Mayan jigsaw have led some commentators to the conclusion that our apparently 'superior knowledge' about the human condition – our place in the universe, the truth about cycles of existence – has always existed. It is as if a parallel stream of knowledge, known only by some, has run alongside the relative ignorance of the struggling masses. Could it be that this hidden knowledge about our common fate, our common inheritance, is finally being made known to us through the wisdom of the Mayan calendar?

*The head of a priest emerges from a feathered serpent's mouth, another expression of Quetzalcoatl. This stone artefact comes from the Puuc style of Mayan architecture, dominant in the Late Classic period.*

# Pacal the Great

*It was 1949 when the Mexican archeologist Alberto Ruz Lhuillier first discovered a false floor in the Temple of the Inscriptions at Palenque. On removing the stone slabs, he revealed a stairway that led down into the space within the pyramid, although this passage was blocked by huge amounts of rubble. Nevertheless, Ruz believed he was on the brink of something important. Yet even he could not guess at the treasures that lay beneath him.*

It took three back-breaking years for Ruz and his team to clear the stairway, discovering, as they descended, fragments of pottery, jade and shell. Further down, the stairs changed direction and led to an antechamber where the skeletons of six young men were found. Beyond this was a triangular stone slab barring the way to something Ruz could not, even in his wildest dreams, have imagined. And when the door was finally pulled back, he was overwhelmed.

### Tomb of the god-king

The burial chamber of Palenque's greatest ever ruler, Pacal the Great, was 9 metres (29 feet) long and some 7 metres (23 feet) wide. Around the walls were painted stucco reliefs of figures now believed to be the Nine Lords of the Night. On the floor were two beautiful moulded stucco heads depicting a man and a woman, as well as two other figures in jade. But much more imposing was the huge sarcophagus that dominated the room. And even more stunning to Ruz and his team was the flat stone lid that sealed the tomb, bearing carvings of such strength, subtlety and complexity that they have fascinated Mayanists ever since and have become a universal symbol for the mysterious knowledge of the Maya.

*Pacal's left hand, like the right, was buried with jade rings and a large piece of jade. Like the Chinese, the Maya believed in the restorative, life-affirming power of this semi-precious stone.*

When Ruz's team eventually managed to remove the vast, carved, 5.1-tonne (5-ton) lid, they were stunned to see a decayed figure, its face entirely covered by an eerie green mosaic death-mask made of jade. In fact, jade appeared in every artefact that adorned the figure's body: he wore jade and mother-of-pearl ear-hoops, jade rings, necklaces of jade, and significant pieces of jade had been placed in each of his hands and inside his mouth.

The find was unlike anything hitherto unearthed on the American continent. The discovery was as great as Howard Carter's opening of the Great Pyramid of Cheops and the revelation of Tutankhamun: in another pyramid on the other side of the world, Ruz had discovered another god-king. The jade mask enveloped the face of Pakal II, Pakal the Great. Known by his Mayan name of K'inich Janaab' Pakal, he was ruler of Palenque until his death at the age of 80. Some have also claimed him to be 'Pacal Votan', lineal descendant of the original mythic figure of Votan, and Master of the Maya.

*The origins and meaning of Pacal's tomb lid has been the subject of intense speculation and theorizing for the more than 50 years since its discovery.*

## Pacal the Great's reign

From the many glyphs at Palenque, it has been possible to decode the history of its rulers as well as other factual information. It is now known that Pacal the Great was born in 603, son of the then-queen Lady Zac-Kuk; that he ascended to the throne on his maturity at the age of 12 on 29 July 615; and that he died in 683. In his 80-year life he initiated and oversaw perhaps the greatest cultural flowering of Mayan culture: there were enormous achievements in the arts, architecture and politics during his reign. As well as undertaking massive building programmes at Palenque, Pacal formed great social alliances with other city-states, such as Tikal and Yaxchilan. When he died he was succeeded by his son K'inich Kan B'ahlam II, whose job it was to bury his father in the the pyramid below the Temple of the Inscriptions. B'ahlum II was himself succeeded by his brother Kan Xul II in 702.

## The jade death-mask

The mosaic jade mask is itself a work of great craftsmanship, to which some scholars have attempted to attribute almost supernatural power. Like the stucco heads found in the tomb, the mask is a likeness of Pacal the Great, with a sloping forehead and large mouth. Its eyes are made of white shell, with obsidian pupils of the deepest black. The fact that burial with jade is also an Asian practice has caused some to suggest that there may have been more cultural migration in early times than we might ordinarily think. Indeed, there are scientists who believe that all American peoples originally came from Asia. At the same time there are those who make the case that the Maya people, particularly those who sowed the seeds for the Classic era, were in some way connected with ancient Egypt and with the Lost Continent of Atlantis.

The discovery of Pacal's tomb has only served to increase the number of theories about the origins – natural or supernatural – of the Maya: it was the design on the tomb lid that inspired the Swiss writer Erich von Däniken to put forward his UFO-inspired theories in the 1960s book *Chariots of the Gods*.

Mayan researcher Maurice Cotterell has attempted to show that within the mosaic pattern of Pacal's jade death-mask is a multi-layered pictorial message, which he believes he has decoded. In *The Supergods*, he suggests that the mask hides a remarkable story:

> *So here we have a jade mask covering the face of a man in a tomb, buried beneath a pyramid in the rainforests of Central America. It conceals a strange story suggesting that the man on the one hand was the giver of life and yet on the other took life away. It tells us this man was the feathered serpent who fought evil to rule the sky and that his opposite number is sacrifice. Yet no human being could have encoded so much incredible information into this jade jigsaw puzzle. So who, or what, did?*

*Removed from its original location in the Temple of the Inscriptions, Pacal's death mask now forms a central exhibit in Mexico City's Anthropological Museum.*

# The lid of Palenque

*The magnificent lid of Palenque is the limestone slab measuring 3.5 by 2 metres (11½ by 6½ feet) that covers Pacal the Great's tomb. Too large for the door of the tomb, the lid must have been created and positioned – presumably along with the sarcophagus and tomb room – before the pyramid was built. It is now believed that Pacal designed his own tomb and started its construction in about 675 CE.*

### The lid's image

Mayan scholars generally accept that the main character depicted in the central portion of the lid is Pacal himself. The fact that he is reclining – perhaps falling back – indicates that he is at the point of death, falling into Xibalbá, the underworld, where the death god (clearly portrayed with teeth) awaits him, just as it awaited the Hero Twins. Pacal himself is in the middle world of mortal life, and above him is the upper world of the heavens, where the celestial bird flies. Running from top to bottom is the tree of life or world tree (see page 54), with its roots in the underworld and its upper branches in the heavens. Pacal is falling into the realm of death, but he will (like Christ) be resurrected. Mayan mythology is very clear that death is not the end – particularly for someone as important as the ruler of Palenque. This is reinforced by those who suggest that the imagery and accompanying glyphs actually depict the birth of Pacal, rather than his death.

### Cotterell's interpretation

While Maurice Cotterell acknowledges that Pacal was indeed a god in human clothing – a kind of avatar or Christ figure, not just for the Maya people, but for all human cultures that followed him – he does not believe, ironically, that the figure on the tomb lid is a representation of Pacal. Instead, he has argued that the lid reveals the ancient history of the Maya from the beginning of time to the present day. He believes the figures shown on it symbolize both the creation and the destruction of the five great ages of Mayan history.

Cotterell maintains that the central figure is an image of the female creation goddess of water, Chalchiuhtlicue, and that she represents the end of that first Mayan age by flood. The symbolic shapes that surround her are also gods of creation: Ehecoatl, bird-shaped god of air and wind, who signified destruction by storm or hurricane; Tlaloc, six-toothed god of divine fire and rain, signifying destruction wrought by volcanoes; and Tonatiuh, the sun god, with his tongue sticking out, representing destruction by drought.

Cotterell believes the fifth symbol, a jaguar-like image, predicts the annihilation of this current fifth age, the age of the jaguar, at the end of the Long Count calendar, on 22 December 2012. But what does the jaguar symbolize? Does it, in Cotterell's understanding at least, evoke the method by which the Earth will be destroyed? And is it possible that Pacal could have predicted how our age might end? It seems implausible, but perhaps – in this age of uncertainty and fear of climate meltdown – we need to revise our views.

*Few artefacts have generated as much controversy as the lid of Pacal's tomb. Its complex imagery holds an enduring fascination and work to fully decode its meaning continues unabated.*

# José Argüelles

*In the mid-1980s a US-based writer and college teacher named José Argüelles published a book called* The Mayan Factor, *which, for better or worse, attracted a lot of attention to the subject of the Mayan Long Count calendar and the meaning of the 2012 end-date. Argüelles' ideas about the metaphysical meaning of the calendar and the role of Pacal, or 'Pacal Votan' as Argüelles named him, were written in a style that was both vague and complex.*

### The transformational message

In *The Mayan Factor* and subsequent books, such as *The Call of Pacal Votan*, Arguelles appeals to humankind to wake up to the transformational message of the calendar and, in particular, to reject our Gregorian calendar year based on 12 months and 60-minute hours, in favour of the natural 'time science' of the Mayan system based on 13 months of 28 days (364 days), with an extra 'green day' to make up 365 days and some intercalary additions. He argues that the end-date of the Long Count calendar coincides with the end of a 26,000-year cycle in which the Earth is entering a 'Galactic Synchronization Beam' issuing from the centre of the universe, which is changing the 'consciousness frequency' at which human life is experienced.

Through a change in the individual and group consciousnesses of human beings on the planet, Argüelles argues, humankind has the opportunity to help planet Earth take its place within the solar system and the wider galaxy as an enlightened part of creation. 'Big stuff' then! Or, in Argüelles' own words: 'The level of progressive mentation and technological complexification leads the biosphere to a hyper-biomutational adjustment called the transition to the noosphere. The noosphere is brought about by the human component of the biomass understanding time as the fourth dimension, which, by making conscious the unconscious timing frequencies, initiates a new level of conscious planetary self-regulation.'

### The believers and doubters

Argüelles attracted a lot of followers among the New Age community and was instrumental in setting up an event known as the Harmonic Convergence on 16–17 August 1987, during which hundreds of thousands of people gathered at sacred sites around the world to meditate. From Argüelles' perspective, the event was a precursor for the 2012 end-date, the beginning of a window during which humankind had the opportunity to change its focus from the material to the spiritual, in an attempt to alter the Earth's fate.

For many people, Argüelles' writing is impenetrable; to others, it is ridiculous babble; but there are many who take his ideas seriously. Certainly academic Mayan scholars are not keen to give credence to the idea that Pacal the Great was in fact a kind of Christ-like galactic super-being, who appeared in the 7th century in order to leave a message for those who would face the end of the 13th *baktun*, the culmination of the Long Count calendar. They are also not happy to countenance the specific identification of Pacal with the myth of Votan, or the implication that Pacal was in fact Kukulkán, the Mayan version of the sun god Quetzalcoatl.

Argüelles portrays 'Pacal Votan' as a hyper-enlightened being, 'time's special witness', Galactic Agent 13 66 56, whom he says has guided him in all his discoveries. By the specific timing of his sojourn on Earth and his 'cycle of power' between 615 and 683 CE, Pacal demonstrated his 'mastery of Mayan time science'. Argüelles therefore believes that Pacal's mission was to bring humanity back to a time system that is harmonious with the galaxy and, by so doing, avoid the payback for our unnatural ways before it is too late.

While many are sceptical about the almost cult-like aspects of Argüelles' teachings and the popularity he has attracted, there are others who credit him with drawing global attention to the importance of the Maya and the knowledge contained in their calendar.

## Not the end of the world?

It is interesting that recent decodings of the hieroglyphs at Palenque, which are understood to have been made during the reign of Pacal the Great, refer to dates *beyond* the end of the Long Count calendar. On the Tablet of Inscriptions at Palenque, a date of 1.0.0.0.0.8 5 Lamat 1 Mol can be inferred – otherwise known as 21 October 4772, almost 3,000 years in the future. Perhaps we can deduce from this that Pacal himself believed that the end of the fifth age did not represent the end of time or of the Earth, and that his name would still be mentioned in the sixth age.

Susan Milbraath, the curator of Latin American Art and Archeology at the Florida Museum of Natural History, has said: 'We [the archeological community] have no record or knowledge that the Maya would think the world would come to an end' in 2012. There are, however, those who would beg to differ.

*The stucco head from Pacal's tomb is the most lifelike portrait of the god-king that remains from his time. His facial features appear to exemplify Mayan physical beauty.*

# The crystal skulls

*Perhaps the strangest artefacts to have been linked with Mayan knowledge are a group of crystal skulls – models of human skulls, apparently carved from clear quartz crystal and other semi-precious minerals. But what did these beautiful, yet haunting objects mean to the Maya, and what is the source of their continuing fascination? And does the story of how they were discovered by European explorers help to reveal their true meaning?*

### Adventurer extraordinaire

Frederick Albert 'Mike' Mitchell-Hedges was the kind of glamorous and courageous English adventurer who could have inspired the character of Indiana Jones. A passionate archeologist and explorer, he headed for British Honduras (now Belize) in 1924 with a team of explorers from the British Museum's Maya Committee. Sticking true to his motto 'Life which is lived without zest and adventure is not life at all', he went in search of important discoveries and high times. He had a personal belief that the cradle of civilization was not somewhere in the Middle East, but instead existed in the lost continent of Atlantis and its survivors, who had, he thought, had escaped to Central America, where they settled.

*On 6 January 1926, Frederick Albert Mitchell-Hedges left England for Central America to explore and excavate the Mayan city of Lubaantun.*

After heading inland from the port of Punta Gorda, Mitchell-Hedges and his team hit some early setbacks. On the crocodile-ridden Rio Grande, the canoe carrying their medical supplies overturned and sank. Then one of the team contracted malaria and, because he could not be treated, died as a result of the illness. It was only the help of the local Kekchi Maya people that enabled the explorers to make their way into the depths of the old Mayan world. Finally, after much fruitless searching, the group came upon some stone ruins, mostly overgrown with moss and foliage. 'We can't be very far from this lost city,' Mitchell-Hedges is believed to have said.

A year of cutting and clearing, slashing and burning followed. Huge fires of foliage filled the jungle with smoke and ash, but when they eventually subsided, they revealed what the explorer had wished for: the remains of a great Mayan city. Frederick Mitchell-Hedges described the thrill he felt in his 1954 autobiography *Danger, My Ally*:

> *We were amazed at the immensity of the ruins. Walls, terraces and mounds came into view as the holocaust swept onwards… in its centre had stood a mighty Citadel… The Citadel was raised above the level of the surrounding countryside and when it was first built it must have stood out like a glittering snow-white island, one hundred and fifty feet [46 metres] high. Around it spread the lesser dwellings and burial mounds of the common people and, further out, the thousands of acres of green, waving maize that must have been necessary to feed and support the large population.*

The city was larger and more complex than they could have imagined, and finding it represented the beginning of a seven-year excavation of the place that today is known as Lubaantun: 'It covered a total area of six square miles [15.5 sq km] with pyramids, palaces, terraces, mounds, walls houses, subterranean chambers, even a huge amphitheatre

*Buried deep in the jungles of Belize, Lubaantun is unusual for its style of construction. The main buildings, which are curved at their corners, were constructed using a dry mortarless method.*

designed to hold more than 10,000 people and approached by two great stairways. The Citadel was built over seven and a half acres [3 hectares] and originally every foot had been covered with cut white stone...'

## Anna's discovery

Early in the great adventure Mitchell-Hedges was joined by his 16-year-old adopted daughter Anna, or 'Sammy' as she was known to her father. Anna soon settled into the role as a young adventurer and, even at her tender age, was just as fearless as her father. One blisteringly hot day, while everyone else was resting from fatigue, she decided to explore the site on her own: 'I thought this was my chance to go up and see how far I could see from the top of the highest building. Of course, I was strictly forbidden to climb up there because the stones were very loose and dangerous. But I had heard that you could see for miles around from the top of one of the pyramids and that intrigued me.'

Anna climbed the steps of the highest pyramid:

*Once I was up there I could see for miles and it was very beautiful. I felt that I could have stayed there for a very long time. But the sun was very, very strong and there was something shining in my face. Way, way down below through a crack I could see something shining back at me and I got very, very excited. How I got down from that building so quickly I don't know, but when I got back I woke my father up and told him I'd seen something. Then, of course, I got a very bad scolding because I shouldn't have gone up there.*

## 'The most beautiful thing I had ever seen'

Despite initial scepticism, her father began a search of the pyramid. A week later, on Anna's 17th birthday, and after the team had taken sufficient stones away, the young girl was lowered into pyramid:

*I had two ropes tied around my body and a light strapped to my head and I was let down into the opening. As I descended into the dark, I became very nervous because there could be snakes and scorpions down there. When I got down I could still see something shining, reflecting the light on my head back at me. So I picked it up and I wrapped it in my shirt so it wouldn't be hurt and I told them to pull me up as fast as they could.*

Just like a scene from a Hollywood movie, Anna wiped the dirt from the object to reveal 'the most beautiful thing I had ever seen'. It was a brilliant life-sized skull made of the clearest rock crystal, and apparently perfect in every way. Her father lifted the skull high in the air so that all the Mayan assistants could see it. After a moment's silence there was

a stunning reaction: 'All the Maya helpers on the dig started laughing and crying. They kissed the ground and started hugging each other,' Anna reported. '[It was] as if an ancient and powerful force had returned to the lives of those present.' That night the Maya dressed themselves in jaguar skins and macaw feathers and began chanting and singing. 'They performed ceremonies, rituals and dances in front of the skull in the firelight.'

Over the following days the miraculous find attracted Maya people from many miles away. Priests came to study the object, and Anna reported what they said about this very ancient artefact: 'The Mayan priests say it is over 100,000 years old. The Mayans told us the skull was made after the head of a great high priest many, many thousands of years ago because this priest was loved very much and they wanted to preserve their truth and wisdom for ever. The old man said that the skull could be made to talk, but how it was done he wouldn't say.'

So impressed was he by the reverence with which the Maya regarded the remarkable skull that Mitchell-Hedges decided to hand the object back to them. Having discovered it and risked her life to recover it, Anna was less happy at her father's gesture.

## Exquisite art or mystical object?

For the next three years the excavations continued, with many extraordinary artefacts being uncovered. One of these was the lower jaw belonging to the crystal skull, which was quickly united with the original find. In 1927, when the time came for the expedition to

*Skull imagery appears throughout Mayan art and architecture, such as the Tzompantli platform at Chichén Itzá. Death was an ever-present reality for the Maya and a good life could only be by the occurrence of a good death.*

return to England with its booty, Anna was surprised when the Maya with whom she had lived during her time in the jungle decided to give the skull to her father, as a gesture of their gratitude for his generosity during the time he had been with them. Anna was delighted that the skull would still be a part of her life.

Mitchell-Hedges explored and lectured until 1951 when he retired to Farley Castle in Berkshire, where he would regularly regale guests with stories of the 'Skull of Doom' and its aura of evil. Whether or not visitors believed his stories, there were many who were deeply impressed by the craftsmanship involved in such an enigmatic and apparently perfect object. Indeed, when the Mitchell-Hedges' skull was tested in the laboratories of Hewlett-Packard (the computer makers and world experts in crystallography), they could detect not a single tool mark on the surface of the skull. They concluded that the exquisite work on the large piece of rock crystal could have taken the equivalent of 300 man (or woman) years of work. This all challenges the still-prevalent idea that the Maya were some kind of primitive people who lacked sophistication.

In 1959 'Mike' Mitchell-Hedges died, and the skull passed into the sole possession of Anna, who has kept the object in her own safekeeping since then, occasionally allowing serious researchers to have contact with it. Since then many people have claimed that the crystal skull has important powers, that it holds secrets and coded information. Others maintain that it is part of a unique set of crystal skulls that will one day be reunited and form a grid of energy that will have a profound effect on humanity. The origins of the Mitchell-Hedges skull, deep in the jungles of what is now Belize, have stimulated even more theories that the Maya – so advanced in their understanding of cosmology, mathematics and prophecy – created such skulls as part of their communication to future generations. But if this is correct, what are the skulls trying to tell us? What is their meaning, and how will we discover their esoteric knowledge?

## Other crystal skulls

The skull is an image that haunts humankind perhaps more deeply than any other: it appears in the great art of the world in sculpted and painted form; it takes stunning roles in the greatest of our plays; and in Mexico it appears forcefully in annual celebrations. It should not surprise us that it has a universal resonance and that its appearance is filled with meaning and mystery – the mystery of our own mortality.

The 'Mitchell-Hedges skull' is far from being the only crystal skull in existence that claims an ancient history. Although it is impossible to date such skulls accurately using any material analysis, there appear to be other examples that may also have come from the time of the Maya and even further back.

## The British Museum skull

The Museum of Mankind in London, previously part of the British Museum, was the home of a full-sized skull after it bought the object at Tiffany's in New York in 1898. It is now on permanent display in the British Museum itself. The skull's history is obscure, but it is believed to have been brought back from Mexico by a Spanish 'soldier of fortune'. The label on the glass case that held the skull in the Museum of Mankind read: 'Aztec sculpture. Skull of rock of crystal. Mexico. Probably Aztec. C. AD 1300–1500. The style of the piece suggests that it dates from the Aztec period. If, however, as one line of the carving suggests, a jeweller's wheel was used to make the cut, the piece would date from after the Spanish Conquest. Length 21 cm [8¼ in].'

There are those who believe this skull is considerably older than the date given by the British Museum; that (along with the Mitchell-Hedges skull) it is only one of at least 13 ancient full-sized skulls on the planet; and that these skulls relate to prophecies about the end-date of the Mayan calendar and other predictions concerning the future of humanity.

## The Texas skull

Another important example is the skull known as 'Max', now owned by a Texan couple named JoAnn and Carl Park, but previously the property of a Tibetan Buddhist monk named Norbu Chen, who claimed to have been given the sacred object by a Guatemalan shaman.

## The Smithsonian skull

There is also a skull in the Smithsonian National Museum of American History, which is renowned for its ugly appearance and for the theory that it is cursed. The larger-than-life-sized, pale pumpkin-coloured skull was donated to the museum by someone who no longer wanted to be its owner; it arrived at the museum in Washington, DC with a note: 'Dear Sir, This Aztec crystal skull, purporting to be part of the (Mexican President) Porforio Diaz collection, was purchased in Mexico City in 1960... I am offering it to the Smithsonian without any consideration. Naturally I wish to remain anonymous.'

When the museum attempted to track down the owner of the skull, they discovered a trail of tragedy. Only able to find the donor's lawyer, they discovered that the man who bought it had committed suicide. A series of terrible events had befallen him since he had become the skull's steward: his wife had died, his son had been involved in an accident that had left him 'brain-dead' and, to cap it all, he himself had been made bankrupt. After all this, the man had not been able to live with his suffering and took his own life – although not before he had made his donation of the skull to the Smithsonian.

The Smithsonian skull is quite different from many of the other skulls in existence that claim ancient origins, not just because of its orange colour, but because it has hollow eye sockets and is, itself, hollow. It is not precise in its carving and gives an impression of Neanderthal culture rather than that of *Homo sapiens*. It has often failed to endear itself to those who have viewed it – indeed, many people find it 'creepy' or 'weird', and some even refuse to look into its eyes for fear of evil befalling them.

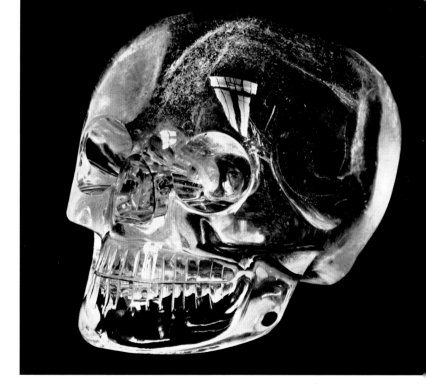

*The crystal skull now on display in the British Museum is the subject of controversy. While many believe it to be Aztec in origin, more sceptical researchers maintain that its origins lie in 19th-century Europe.*

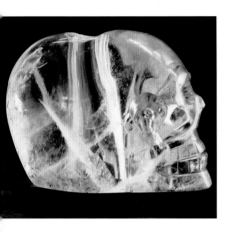

*Above: The Paris skull has a distinct depression in its crown through which a rod, or even – as some believe – a cross could have been placed.*

## The Paris skull

In the Trocadero Museum in Paris, also known as the Musée de l'Homme, lives a smaller crystal skull. Just 11 cm (4⅓ in) high and weighing less than 3 kg (6½ lb), the artefact has no separate jawbone, as the Mitchell-Hedges skull does. For many experts, though, its style is unmistakably Aztec or Mixtec, and holes in the top and base have convinced many that the skull is 'pre-Columbian' and worked by hand, rather than with European tools. The holes, it is thought, would enable the skull to be placed on a stick or rod – also indicating that there may have been a number of skulls, stacked on top of each other.

## The Sha Na Ra skull

A skull named 'Sha Na Ra' belongs to a private collector and psychic named Nick Nocerino, who has had a number of mind-bending experiences with skulls that have led him to believe that they do have a particular power to affect people.

Nocerino says that, when he was a young kid growing up in New York, he looked in the mirror one day to be confronted with the image of a skull, with a snake sliding out of one eye socket and a jaguar coming from the other. And during the Second World War he was fighting in France when a farmer decided that the visiting American was the man to whom he should give a very special object that he treasured. The object was, of course, a clear quartz crystal skull. At the time Nocerino was not in the business of lugging heavy crystal skulls around battlefields and told the Frenchman to keep it safe from advancing German troops. He was never to see the skull again, although there are those who believe it is now in the hands of a French secret society.

As to how Nocerino was able to locate Sha Na Ra, he reports that he found it in the Mexican state of Guerrero using his abilities as a 'psychic archeologist' and a local team of spade-wielding accomplices. Having located the spot, Nocerino joined in on several days of digging before a hidden tomb yielded its treasure.

Like many crystal-skull devotees, Nocerino now works psychically with Sha Na Ra, channelling information that he claims is locked up in the crystal structure of the skull, awaiting a sensitive mind such as his. He has also worked with many other skulls – a rose-quartz skull, an amethyst skull and the Mitchell-Hedges skull – to reveal different kinds of information, some about the past, some about the future.

### Repositories of nightmare or prophecy?

Nocerino says that sensitives who work with skulls often claim to see a particular set of images on their first contact. These are, traditionally, images of great change: volcanic eruptions, earthquakes rocking cities, giant tsunamis laying waste to the land, forests crashing down, tectonic plates shifting. Some believe this set of nightmare visions may relate to the origins of crystal skulls prior to the destruction of ancient Atlantis. Others believe the skulls offer a prophecy of the end of our current age in December 2012.

Nocerino's own take on his experiences is less definite. He believes that the skulls are so old that they store the knowledge of events going back many tens of thousands of years and, by offering their knowledge of history, present us with a chance to react differently, grow spiritually and avoid the global disasters of the past as we move into the cycles of the future.

*Right: At Palenque, the Temple of the Dead, or the Temple of the Skull as it is also known, is decorated with this dramatic carved image.*

## Prophecy-channelling and skull wisdom

Nick Nocerino is not the only psychic who claims to have channelled information from ancient crystal skulls. These days there is no shortage of channellers and psychics ready to bring forth the secret information with which they say the skulls are encoded.

One source of knowledge about the skulls, which has attracted interest and controversy, are the Native Americans of North America. In her book *The 13 Original Clan Mothers*, author and wisdom teacher Jamie Sams retells the legend of the 13 Clan Mothers who came to planet Earth to assist humanity in its evolution. Sams is of Seneca, Cherokee and French descent, and her portrayal of the Clan Mothers emerges from contact with her Native American elders. The 13 Clan Mothers each gave a particular quality to those they taught and, when their mission was over and they departed, they left their wisdom and knowledge encoded within 13 crystal skulls to which people would have access. Sams' legend has no date; it simply reverberates from the deep past.

Although she has been criticized for her revelations of native wisdom, Sams' interpretation of the meaning of the skulls transcends other mundane ideas:

> *The crystal skulls symbolize transformation on many levels. For not only is the skull a symbol of the transformation we can experience in physical death, but it is a symbol of the transformation that is available to us in life. If we know that to die physically is not the end, then we can see that all the other 'endings' we fear in our lives are new beginnings… Once we no longer fear death we are able to see that all changes in our lives are part of the constant cycle of death and rebirth. Each moment, as something in us dies, something else can be reborn.*

Sams also maintains that the Aztecs, who were once the holders of the crystal skulls, misused and misunderstood their power. At another time it was a group of Native North Americans who kept the skulls in a lodge, where the light of fires would pass through the skulls, generating rainbows around the room, representing a microcosm of the Earth and all who lived on it.

## Otherworldly origins

The Native Americans may have reverenced the skulls, as they reverenced the Earth, Sams says, but the original source of the skulls was not even this planet. Like other people before her, Sams maintains that the skulls were created somewhere else in the universe and brought here by 'sky gods', whose aim was to teach humanity more about its spiritual and consciousness potential. They came at a time when the human skull had been growing to a point where many women were dying in childbirth; this was happening to such a degree that the future of the human species was threatened.

She also claims that, in the stories of her Native American elders, *Homo sapiens* does not simply represent the Darwinian evolution of humans from an earlier state as

Neanderthals and other hominids. In fact, *Homo sapiens* is a genetic combination of the sky gods and Neanderthals. This theory does at least partially address the problematic 'missing link' between early hominids and *Homo sapiens* (as human beings are known in anthropaleontology). When the 'sky gods' came from other planets, Sams maintains, the crystal skulls they brought with them contained knowledge from each of the different source planets and star systems. They represented a storehouse of all the important wisdom and information – mathematics, astronomy, philosophy and science – that was needed for a new, spiritually evolved line of terrestrial humanity to develop and flourish.

If such a radical and – to some people – outrageous theory were true, we might think that the human race has both spectacularly succeeded and ignominiously failed.

*Recovered from the Templo Mayor in the centre of Mexico City in 1978, the Coyolxauhqui stone depicts the eponymous goddess naked and dismembered. On her waistband she clearly carries the skull of a previous victim.*

## The Maya and the skulls

We have heard what Europeans and North Americans believe about the crystal skulls; we know a bit more about the psychics and scientists who have investigated these extraordinary artefacts with unknown origins. But what do the indigenous Maya people who still live in the lands of the Classic Maya believe about the skulls? What do they know of their purpose, and how do they fit into the Mayan spiritual perspective of life? Even more importantly, do the skulls have anything to tell us about the end of the Mayan calendar in December 2012?

Hunbatz Men is a Mayan Daykeeper, a shaman and a representative of the Itzá tradition that is still prominent in the Yucatán peninsula. He is based in Mérida, close to the famous Mayan site of Chichén Itzá, but travels regularly to organize and officiate at ceremonies and rituals that maintain and renew Mayan sacred life. He comes from an unbroken family line of sacred wisdom teachings that dates back more than 500 years.

As well as representing the enduring truths of Mayan culture, Hunbatz Men maintains that the crystal skulls have a special significance in the history of his people. He claims that Itzam Ná, commonly known as a god within the Mayan pantheon, gave the Maya people the knowledge of what the skulls represent and how they are to be used in the sacred centres of the Mayan world.

Hunbatz Men says that the skulls and their physical proportions tell of the Maya's sacred connection with their god Hunab K'u. He feels that while the sacred skulls have had an influence on the world by being taken to different places, it is now time – as the end of the calendar approaches – for the skulls to return to the Mayan sacred centres. Interviewed for a film about the crystal skulls by Ceri Louise Thomas and Chris Morton, Hunbatz Men explained their importance at this time:

*Stela 35 at Yaxchilan depicts the ruler Lady Xoc (or Skull-Ik as she is also known) experiencing a mystical vision while she holds a skull in her right hand.*

*As it was prophesied, the rest of humanity, it began to take the skulls from our sacred centres and then they were sleeping for a while. But now it is good to send us back the skulls for our sacred centres, because we need the skulls to activate each sacred centre in all the areas of the Maya. Because now it is necessary for all humanity to wake up... Let them give us the skulls to re-establish them in our sacred centres, because that's another part of the prophecy. We need the skulls again to establish in our sacred pyramids... and then the others will come.*

## Learning respect for Mother Earth

Hunbatz Men's campaign to bring the skulls back as part of a global education process goes on apace. He regularly holds ceremonies at Chichén Itzá, Tikal and other major Mayan sites where crystal skulls play an important role by their presence. The idea of the return of Kukulkán or Quetzalcoatl is not, for this Mayan Daykeeper, a remote dream. Instead he sees that we – humanity – are the carrier of the Christ-like, Buddha-like presence of Kukulkán. Through our developing relationship with sacred knowledge, we can become more and express more of this living presence: 'From this moment on, I would like you to realize that we are all Quetzalcoatl or Kukulkán. We need only to develop our faculties of consciousness to fully realize that status.'

The skulls are there to energize this process, Hunbatz Men thinks, and to keep us on track. For him, their part in the process is essential:

*Ceremonial axe from the Late Classic period shows an eagle or a vulture perched on a skull with its jaw opened.*

*...the work we're going to do now, the Maya are now beginning to do some work, to give everyone this information. Because the information from the skulls can help the human beings to wake up and then begin to see the mistakes they're making on the Mother Earth. Because what we need now is more respect for the Mother Earth, because with the respect we can begin to understand the process of the Mother Earth, the normal changes of the Mother Earth.*

*And we need the skulls because humanity now, it must wake up. Because if humanity does not wake up, then we will kill the Mother Earth and there is nowhere else we can live...*

As a link to ancient Mayan wisdom, Hunbatz Men is playing a vital role in educating modern Western humans about the significance of this time and the challenges it offers. We may be wise to listen.

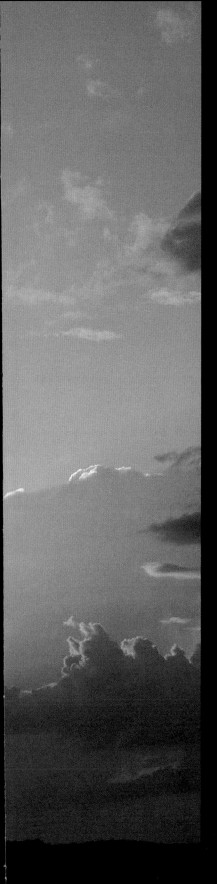

## Chapter 7

# A NEW DAWN OR ENDLESS NIGHT?

So what should we expect when we wake up on 21 December 2012? In the northern hemisphere it will be the darkest day of the year, but will it be a day of true darkness for all humanity or one of transformation? Or will it be, as some believe, a day like any other?

The answer to this question could be a very individual one. For most people, it is difficult to relate our own mortality to the mortality of the human race or the condition of the Earth. In the Western world we live separate lives, largely unaffected by the major events that can devastate whole communities. Yet we know that many people have lived through such overwhelming experiences – tsunamis, floods, eruptions, earthquakes and world wars exist within our memories.

The way we view such events is greatly affected by our spiritual perspective on life. If we believe that mortal, material life is all we have, then death and destruction truly are the end of our individual (and possibly our collective) identities. If, however, we sense that death is not the end and that a part of us lives on, we may view impending events as part of a spiritual initiation, a cosmic challenge to our ability to resist fear. For perhaps it is not events that we should fear, but fear itself. For is it not fear that causes us to behave in ways that demean our spirit and makes us lose touch with our ability to express love? Perhaps, then, the question that remains is: how should we prepare for change?

# Transformation and change

*As we come to end of our explorations we need to ask: how well do the prophecies of the Mayan end-date match up with other ideas about unfavourable conditions in the heavens?*

Astrologer Raymond Mardyks has attempted to demonstrate that as many as five different and unusual celestial events will converge in 2012. The first is a transit of Venus across the sun from our perspective. These transits occur in 'pairs', with two transits happening eight years apart, but then not happening again for another 120 years or so. While the next transit will occur during on 5 and 6 June 2012, taking around seven hours to complete, previous transits have occurred in 2004, 1882, 1874, 1769 and 1761.

The second event is a solar eclipse on 20 May 2012, which also 'conjuncts' with the Pleiades star system and with the zenith passage of the sun at Chichén Itzá.

Further events cited by Mardyks include: a second solar eclipse which will happen on 13th November 2012, just one day before an Aztec fire ceremony that will mark the end of a Calendar Round; an alignment of the solstice sun with the Galactic Equator which will complete in 2012; and a return of Venus to the area of the Pleiades constellation. While these events are not necessarily sufficient to cause a rupture in the heavens, their occurrence may not be without significance.

## Crustal displacement and cataclysm

In his well-known book *Fingerprints of the Gods*, Graham Hancock puts forward the theory that a very particular planetary alignment will occur on 24 December 2011. Hancock proposed this date as the moment when the alignment will cause the crust of the Earth, top-heavy with polar ice, to slide out of place and create giant tidal waves that will destroy all life on Earth. At the time he proposed this date, Hancock also believed this was the true date of the end of the Mayan Long Count calendar. However, we now know – from our better understanding of the correlation between our Gregorian calendar and the Mayan calendar – that the end of the 13-*baktun* cycle occurs on 21 December 2012.

In their own book *The Orion Prophecy*, Patrick Geryl and Gino Rainckx put forward the theory that 2012 will witness a global catastrophe initiated by an alignment of planets and stars in exactly the same configuration as occurred in 9792 BCE. This date, the authors claim, was the precise time of a previous cataclysm that saw the destruction of the continent of Atlantis and the flight of the Atlanteans to Central America, South America and Egypt.

*Special events in the heavens, such as solar eclipses, have always been looked on with concern and even trepidation. For many cultures they have acted as a reminder that there are universal powers beyond human control.*

The alignment of stars (including Venus), the authors say, together with changes in the sun's activity, will cause the Earth's magnetic fields to reverse completely in a short time. This will lead to earthquakes, landslides, volcanic eruptions and tsunamis that will engulf the great majority of humanity, demolish all structures and destroy all evidence of our culture. Only by preparing ourselves now, they suggest, can we hope to survive such Earth changes – even then, our chances will be very slim.

The authors of *The Orion Prophecy* have picked up on Maurice Cotterell's ideas about sunspot theory as put forward in *The Mayan Prophecies* and have combined its conclusions, together with mathematical decoding of their own, to come up with a theory that they believe proves there will be a disastrous cataclysm on 21 December 2012.

They also make the claim that the Dresden Codex Venus table (see page 112) is not simply a record of the cycles of Venus, but also contains predictions of sunspot cycles of 187.2 years in duration, or 68,302 days. It turns out that 20 of these sunspot cycles make up the number 1,366,040, the number that Cotterell refers to as his own 'super number', just 520 days less than the 'Maya Great Number' of 1,366,560 contained within the Venus table of the Dresden Codex.

*Lintel 14 at Yaxchilan portrays Lady Large Skull and Bird Jaguar IV commemorating their son's birth in a self-sacrificial ceremony. The Mayans often employed ritual sacrifice and bloodletting in an effort to maintain cosmic order.*

## A concordance of events

The sunspot cycle of 187.2 years is not significant enough on its own to create calamities – otherwise we would expect a cataclysm every time the sun reached its peak of activity. But, the authors of *The Orion Prophecy* say, when this is combined with the fact that the Earth is at a key point in a 12,000-year cycle since the previous cataclysm, it is significant. When it also correlated with the fact that the Earth is at exactly the same status in its 26,000-year precessional cycle, which sees the axis of the Earth tilt changing as it goes around the centre of the galaxy, then the concordance of factors makes a disaster very much more likely.

In the end, of course, all these ideas concerning events around 21 December 2012 are simply theories. Fortunately – or unfortunately, depending on one's viewpoint – most of us will live to find out whether any of them has any basis in fact.

## Natural cycles

As we have seen, the Maya have always believed in the power of Nature, and in the power of her cycles – powers that we (in our over-industrialized and mechanized world) have lost touch with. Our 'modern' calendar of irregular months only bears an approximate relationship to the real meaning of 'months' as moon periods. The hubris of two Romans – Julius Caesar and Pope Gregory XIII, who gave us the Julian and Gregorian calendars – saw to that.

The complex cycles of the Mayan calendar, their wheels within wheels, have a real relationship with important celestial events. With modern science it is now possible to see that there are cycles within our own galaxy that are affecting conditions on our planet. The cycle of solar flares and solar activity affects the Earth's magnetic fields. We are currently

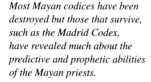

*Most Mayan codices have been destroyed but those that survive, such as the Madrid Codex, have revealed much about the predictive and prophetic abilities of the Mayan priests.*

undergoing a process of magnetic reversal – a process that has happened many times before, but never perhaps under the conditions that the Earth is currently enduring.

Authors and researchers have investigated some of the alternative histories of the planet, histories that appear to reveal that the Earth has undergone great and cataclysmic changes before – changes that echo the different ages in which the Maya and the Aztecs believed. According to these accounts, conditions on Earth have not represented one long party, and we should not expect them to be so different as time moves on.

## Changing perceptions of mutability

We need to remember that the idea of continental drift and the theory of plate tectonics were only put forward in the 1960s. Prior to this it was believed that the great continents were fixed elements on the surface of the Earth. It is as if our discoveries are pulling the metaphorical and continental rug out from under our feet. This huge new understanding of our mutability is almost brand-new; it seems to echo Galileo's discovery that the Earth moves around the sun – both discoveries that were thought, in their time, to be an insult to our fixed notions of ourselves. As the poet and dramatist T.S. Eliot said, 'Man cannot bear too much reality.' Indications of our mortality are rarely welcomed, even though they hold a strange fascination for us.

So it is with the end of the Mayan calendar. If the Maya were so sophisticated, so literally 'ahead of their time', could they really have sent a message down through time to warn us of the dangers we face, of the wisdom we need to understand, of the risks we face by ignoring our spiritual origins?

*The Maya worshipped the rain god Chac because they understood the human consequences of his wrath. He was often portrayed abstractly, as here at Uxmal where his image appears hundreds of times on different buildings.*

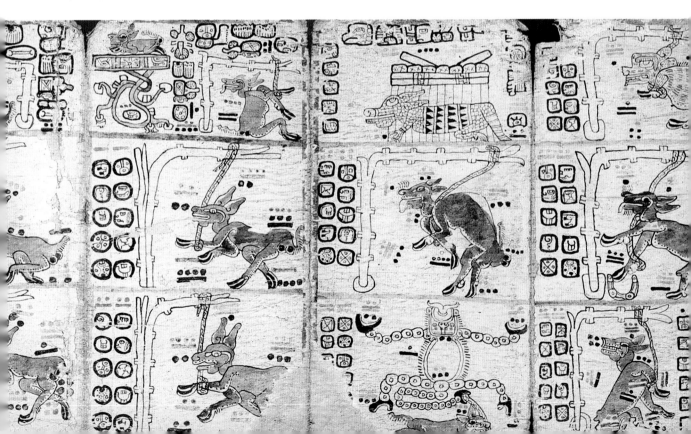

# The Mayan tradition today

*The voice of the Classic Maya lives on. It speaks to us through their art, their architecture, their calendar, their literature. It also speaks through the living human culture of the Maya people who still inhabit Central America and express something of the spirituality that inspired the Maya to greatness more than a thousand years ago. So how do contemporary Maya view the coming end of the Long Count?*

### Facing the challenges of our age

Mayan spiritual leaders such as Hunbatz Men and Don Alejandro Cirilo Perez Oxlaj may offer us relevant wisdom about how to approach such 'interesting times'. Hunbatz Men has spoken of the challenges of this age:

> *Hunab K'u, who can see and understand everything, knows that the time for the great change has come. The word for us to return to the ancient temples has been received from the cosmos. It is here and now that the great Spirit is beginning to call us back to the magnetic sites. The incarnated Masters are beginning to raise their voices of knowledge in the ancient sites that the cosmic word to attain wisdom in a gradual manner has been received.*

He envisages a time of spiritual awakening for those who may not even expect it:

> *Cosmic education will commence again at the crossing of abandoned roads. In forgotten lands the ancient temples will flourish again, the white roads of the High Initiation will be walked on again, roads leading south, north, west, and east. Thousands of people will walk these roads under the celestial vault, heading for the point where the sun rises, awaiting the solar wind. They will hear the solar wind whisper by night, speak with the trees, move as the breeze through dwellings to purify the sceptics, give movement to the clouds, and, when the solar wind reaches*

*At Chichén Itzá the equinoxes are still celebrated by thousands of people who feel a connection to the prescient wisdom of the Maya.*

*those people, it will gently touch their faces to let them know that it is
time for the initiation that will come from the sea and from the sky.*

Hunbatz Men's message is one of respect for the Earth and for the elements, one that has
echoes with the growing environmental movement in the Western world:

*It is to you, Solar Brother or Sister, wherever on earth you may live,
that a brother from the sacred land of the Maya is speaking, to inform
you that the Mayan Spiritual teachers, who dwell in the sacred
pyramids, have directed that we must unite to walk the path of the light
of wisdom, learn again from the wind, the water, the trees, and the sun,
and return to the wisdom of life-giving Mother Earth. These spiritual
Mayan teachers further request that we are to observe solar ethics to
remain as children of the Great Father Sun so that, through our
children and the children of our children, we can exist eternally.*

*It is important that you study the sacred earth, where body and spirit
live in harmony, and, through meditation, rites and sacred chants, ask
Mother Earth the name of the original dwellers of the area where you
now reside. If for some reason you do not obtain an answer, ask the
stones, the trees and the animals who those people were, and, when
you have their name, announce to them with great respect that a
school will be established in that area for the purpose of revealing the
mysteries of the knowledge deposited by them in that sacred area.*

## A time of awakening

Don Alejandro Cirilo Perez Oxlaj works with the crystal skulls and brings knowledge of the
spiritual ways of the Maya to a broader audience . His vision is of a time of positive spiritual
transformation for those who embrace the challenge to 'awaken':

*... the prophecy says the elders will return. The prophecy says now is the
time of the awakening. This is your job now, to awaken. The Vale of the
Nine Hells is past and the Time of the Warning has now arrived. It is time
to prepare for the Age of Thirteen Heavens. The time of 12 Baktun and
13 Ahau is fast approaching, and they shall be here among you to defend
Mother Earth. The prophecy says 'Let the dawn come. Let all the people
and all the creatures have peace, let all things live happily', for the love
must not only be between humans, but between all living things.*

# Bibliography

Argüelles, José, *The Mayan Factor*, Rochester: Bear & Co., 1987

Aveni, Anthony F., *Skywatchers of Ancient Mexico*, Austin: University of Texas Press, 2001

Brinton, Daniel G., *The Maya Chronicles*, Philadelphia: 1882

Closs, M.P., *Mechanism in the Venus Tables of the Dresden Codex: Native American astronomy*, Austin: University of Texas Press, 1977

Christenson, Allen J. (trans.), *Popol Vuh: Literal poetic version, translation and transcription*, Norman: University of Oklahoma Press, 2004

Christenson, Allen J. (trans.), *Popol Vuh: The sacred book of the Maya*, Norman: University of Oklahoma Press, 2003

Coe, M.D., *Breaking the Maya Code*, London: Penguin, 1994

Coe, M.D., *The Maya*, London: Thames & Hudson, 1993

Cotterell, Maurice, *The Amazing Lid of Palenque*: Brooks Hill Perry and Co., 1994

Cotterell, Maurice, *The Mural of Bonampak*: Brooks Hill Perry & Co., 1995

Cotterell, Maurice, *The Supergods*, London: HarperCollins, 1997

Cotterell, Maurice and Gilbert, Adrian, *The Mayan Prophecies*, London: Element Books, 1995

Diamond, Jared, *Collapse*, London: Penguin, 2005

Hancock, Graham, *Fingerprints of the Gods*, Oxford: Heinemann, 1995

Hapgood, C., *Earth's Shifting Crust*, Philadelphia: Chilton Book Co., 1958

Kelley, David, *Deciphering the Maya Script*, Austin: University of Texas, 1976

de Landa, Diego, *Relación de las Cosas de Yucatán/The Relationship of the Things of the Yucatan*, Madrid: Dastin, 2002

de Landa, Diego (trans. Alfred M. Tozze), *Relación de las Cosas de Yucatán: A translation*, Papers of the Peabody Museum of American Archaeology and Ethnology, Harvard University, vol. 18, 1941

de Landa, Diego (trans. William Gates), *Yucatan Before and After the Conquest*, Mineola: Dover Publications, 1978

Love, Bruce, 'A Dresden Codex Mars Table?', *Latin American Antiquity*, 1995, 6:4, pp.350–361

Makemson, M.W., 'The Astronomical Tables of the Maya', *Contributions to American Anthropology and History*, 1943, 42, pp.187–221

Malstrom, V.H., 'Origin of the Mesoamerican 260-Day Calendar', *Science*, 1973, 181, pp.939–941

Men, Hunbatz, *Secrets of Mayan Science/Religion*, Rochester: Bear & Co., 1989

Morley, Sylvanus Griswold, *The Ancient Maya*, Stanford: Stanford University Press, 1994

Morton, Chris and Thomas, Ceri Louise, *The Mystery of Crystal Skulls*, London: Element Books, 1994

Roys, Ralph L., *The Book of Chilam Balam of Chumayel*, Washington: Carnegie Institution of Washington, 1933

Sahagún, Bernardino de (trans. Charles E. Dibble and Arthur J.O. Anderson), *Historia General de las Cosas de Nueva Espana (The Florentine Codex: General History of the Things of New Spain*, vols. 1–12, Santa Fe, NM and Salt Lake City: School for American Research and the University of Utah Press, 1950–82

Sams, Jamie, *The Thirteen Original Clan Mothers*, San Francisco: HarperCollins 1994

Schele, Linda and Friedel, David, *A Forest of Kings*, London: William Morrow, 1990

Stephens, John (illus. Frederick Catherwood), *Incidents of Travel in Central America, Chiapas and Yucatán*, New York: Harper & Brothers, 1841

Stephens, John (illus. Frederick Catherwood), *Incidents of Travel in Yucatán*, New York: Harper & Brothers, 1843

Stray, Geoff, *Beyond 2012: Catastrophe or Ecstasy*, Lewes: Vital Signs Publishing, 2005

Taube, Karl, *Aztec and Mayan Myths*, London: British Museum Press, 1993

Tedlock, Dennis (trans.), *Popol Vuh: The definitive edition of the Mayan book of the dawn of life and the glories of gods and kings*, New York: Simon & Schuster, 1985

Velikovsky, I., *Worlds in Collision*, London: Abacus Books, 1972

Wilcox, Joan Parisi, *Keepers of the Ancient Knowledge*, London: Element Books, 1999

Willson, R.W., *Astronomical Notes on the Maya Codices*, Papers of the Peabody Museum of American Archaeology and Ethnology, Harvard University, vol. 6, no. 3, 1924

## Webography

Fisher, Suzanne D., M.A., and Fisher, Bruce S., Ph.D., The Chilam Balam and the Popol Vuh:
http://myweb.cableone.net/subru/Mayan.html

Finley, Michael, 'The Real Maya Prophecies':
http://members.shaw.ca/mjfinley/mainmaya.html

Foundation for the Advancement of Mesoamerican Studies, Inc. (FAMSI), for the Dresden, Madrid, Grolier and Paris codices: www.famsi.org

Peden, Robert D., 'The Mayan Calendar – Why 260 Days?':
www.spiderorchid.com/mesoamerica/mesoamerica.htm

# Index

Page numbers in *italics* refer to illustrations/captions

# Acknowledgements

## Photographic acknowledgements

With thanks to Coordinación Nacional de Asunto Jurídicos del Instituto Nacional de Antropología e Historia, Mexico.

akg-images 150–151; Bildarchiv Steffens 137; 68–69; Francois Guenet 50; Erich Lessing 52, 61, 63, 82, 118–119, 145

Alamy Ancient Art and Architecture 116; Bruce Coleman Inc 127; Cosmo Condina 6–7; Mary Evans Picture Library 59; © M. Timothy O'Keefe 115; (c) Phototake Inc 17; © Chuck Place 100; The Print Collector 11, 85; Visual Arts Library (London) 70, 72, 77

Ancient Art and Architecture: 8, 93, 152–3

The Art Archive Biblioteca National Madrid/Gianni Dagli Orti 103; National Anthropological Museum Mexico/Gianni Dagli Orti 1 & 55, 125; Gianni Dagli Orti 31; Mexican National Library/Mireille Vautier 89; Mireille Vautier 56.

The Bridgeman Art Library British Museum, London 57

Corbis Diego Azubel/epa 20; Bowers Museum of Cultural Art 62; Gianni Dagli Orti 143; Macduff Everton 47; Bertrand Gardel/Hemis 45; Danny Lehman 94–95; Charles & Josette Lenars 87, 96; NSO/SEL/Roger Ressmeyer 16; Matthieu Paley 21; Keren Su 22; Werner Foreman 53, 113, 122

Getty Images DEA/G Dagli Orti 24–5; DEA/M Borchi 135; Hulton Archive 134; Kenneth Garrett 39; Michael Langford 15

Rex Features Roger Viollet 139, 140

South American Pictures 40; Marion Morrison 88, 110, 130, Tony Morrison 101; Iain Pearson 34; Chris Sharp 105, 121, 133

David Douglas 2, 33, 9, 27, 32, 33, 35, 38, 46, 58, 60, 64, 65, 66, 67, 91, 106, 107, 108, 109, 111, 120, 123, 126, 129, 141, 144, 149, 151 above

Topfoto British Museum/HIP 4 & 26; 18, 148

Werner Foreman Archive 12, 48–49, 146–147; Anthropology Museum, Veracruz University, Jalapa 28; British Museum 97; Museum of Americas, Madrid 42; N J Saunders14; Museum für Volkerkunde, Berlin 51, 99.

## Publisher acknowledgements

Every reasonable effort has been made to trace copyright holders of the following extracts. The publisher apologises for any errors or omissions and would be grateful if notified of any corrections that should be incorporated in future reprints or editions of this book.

p.4: From the Popol Vuh, translated by Suzanne D. Fisher M.A., Instructor of Spanish at Yavapai Community College, Prescott, Arizona, and Bruce S. Fisher, Ph.D.

p.10: From 'The Mayan Worldview of the Universe' by Patrisia Gonzales and Roberto Rodriguez, The Denver Post, January 2, 2000

pp.11, 12, 13: Quoted by permission from Beyond 2012: Catastrophe or Ecstasy by Geoff Stray, Vital Signs Publishing, UK, 2005, pp.29, 35, 37–38

pp.66, 100, 102, 109, 121: From the Chilam Balam, translated by Suzanne D. Fisher M.A., Instructor of Spanish at Yavapai Community College, Prescott, Arizona, and Bruce S. Fisher, Ph.D.

p.58: From an article by Professor Mary Miller published on www.yale.edu.

p.76: From The Maya by Michael D. Coe, Thames & Hudson Ltd., London. © 1966, 1980, 1984, 1987, 1993, 1999 and 2004 Michael D. Coe. Reprinted by kind permission of Thames & Hudson.

p.128: Reprinted by permission of HarperCollins Publishers Ltd © Maurice Cotterell, 1997

p.132: From The Mayan Factor by José Argüelles, Rochester, VT 05767 Copyright © 1987, 1996 Inner Traditions / Bear & Co. www.BearandCompany.com

pp.135–136: From Danger My Ally, F.A. Mitchell-Hedges, 1995 Mitchell-Hedges and Honey, www.mitchell-hedges.com

pp.136, 142, 145, 152, 153: Reprinted by permission of HarperCollins Publishers Ltd © Chris Morton and Ceri Louise Thomas, 1994

**Executive editor** Sandra Rigby
**Senior editor** Fiona Robertson
**Deputy art director** Karen Sawyer
**Designers** Claire Dale and Rebecca Johns/Cobalt
**Illustrator** Peter Liddiard @ Sudden Impact
**Picture research** Claire Gouldstone
**Production controller** Hannah Burke